AF477800

BASIM MAGDY

TO HYPNOTIZE THEM WITH FORGETFULNESS

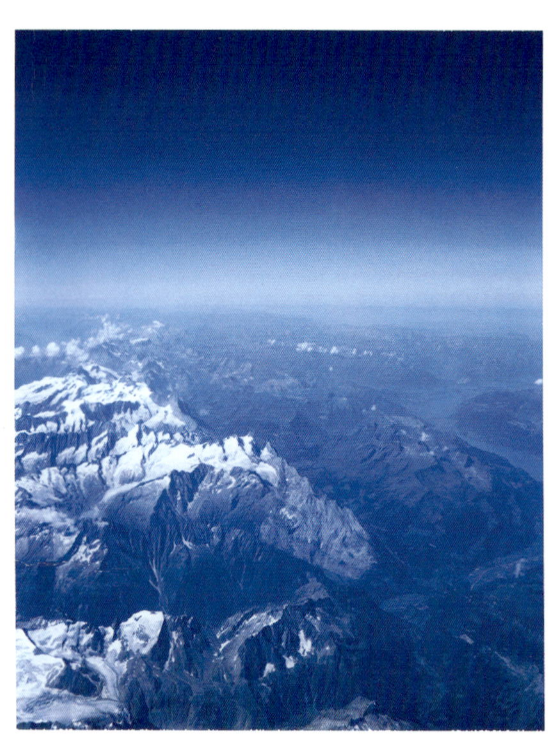

CONTENTS

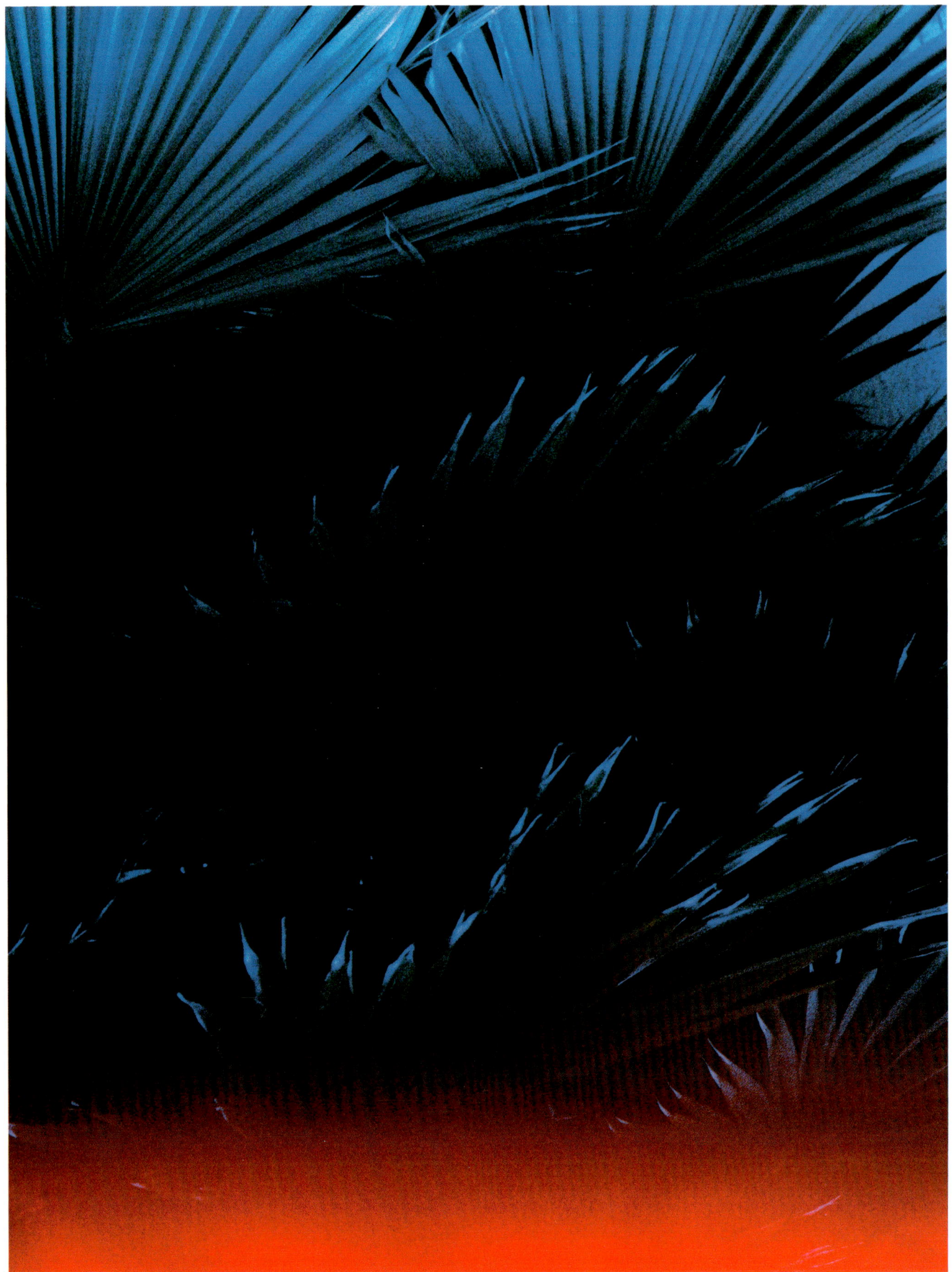

ONLY STONE, BRONZE AND THE SKY SHALL OUTLIVE ALL THE REST.

An excerpt from the script of *The Many Colors of the Sky Radiate Forgetfulness*, 2014.

7 ESSENTIAL THOUGHTS FOR UNDERSTANDING BASIM MAGDY'S REIMAGINATION OF THE CAMERA ARTS
BRUCE JENKINS

In spring 2002, the editors of the journal *October* released a special issue to mark the publication's one-hundredth edition.[1] Its focus was "obsolescence," a theme that contained a trace of vestigial Y2K anxiety while equally acknowledging a tautological dilemma: a cultural journal focused on the most advanced developments within its four declared domains (art, theory, criticism, politics) was nevertheless reaching the century edition of its publication. Would the pronouncements of its first quarter-century become obsolete? The particular set of concerns that became the focal point of twenty-one artist questionnaire responses, a pair of critical roundtables, and essays by leading experts in design and architecture was summoned forth from then-current events within contemporary art and, in particular, the threatening specter of new media and the "*über*-archive of the database," with their totalizing ambitions, poised to overwhelm contemporary art and its discourse.

An old friend of the journal was brought in to lead the counterattack—Walter Benjamin, aided by his sturdy assistant, the "Angel of History." A veteran of one of the first such incursions by technological apparatuses into the realm of art making, the German cultural historian and theorist had ably deployed a somewhat counterintuitive logic, embracing not the new but the debris and wreckage left by the "storm . . . we call progress."[2] What emerged from *October*'s early twenty-first-century engagement with the specter of a technocratic future for the culture was a series of positions that echoed Benjamin's embrace of the "outmoded." Two of these insights achieved impressive degrees of relevance for the current moment: "an embrace of cast-off objects poised against the functional imperatives of contemporary design" and "an intensified mining of the history and specificity of now putatively discarded mediums salvaged from the teeth of their eradication." The editors ended on a hopeful note, embracing the emergent new form of artistic practice "as a site of resistance."[3]

PAINTING BY OTHER MEANS

It is at this particular art-historical juncture that a Cairo-based Egyptian art student named Basim Magdy entered the field, initially engaged in painting. During his five years in art school, Magdy led something of a double life—dutifully painting from plaster models in the classroom (the size of his canvases expanding each year) and producing what he describes as "big angry paintings" at home.[4] A number of these would show up as backdrops in his early portrait paintings, which appear to be set in the artist's studio and include numerous artworks on the walls that more than measure up to his stark description. Magdy, however, began to suffer from an age-old dilemma endemic to the medium: he wanted the static objects in his paintings to move. And so he hired an animator to pixelate his drawings, a process that led to his earliest film, the Flash animation short *Two Days to Apocalypse* (2003). This episodic work is populated by male protagonists, some of whom endure various forms of personal humiliation and others who perform random acts of violence upon a cartoonish world populated by Bart Simpson (beheaded), Superman (gunned down midair), and E.T.[5] Magdy found another outlet for liberating himself from the stasis of the canvas in his early installation work, which expanded the sensory reach of his art by including real objects and props as well as floors laden with sound-inducing material.

But as curator Regine Basha has noted, incipient components of his filmmaking were already visible in Magdy's early paintings and drawings, establishing a medial teleology in which photography and filmmaking ultimately would prove necessary to accomplishing key aspects of his artistic enterprise.[6] We might say, then, that the arc of Magdy's career resembles an aesthetic instance of the

German naturalist Ernst Haeckel's claims about "ontogeny recapitulating phylogeny." For in little more than a decade, the artist would shift from the traditional mediums of the visual arts (painting, drawing, works on paper) to more contemporary modes of art making, thereby retracing an artistic pathway that had unfolded over centuries and emerged fully only in the final decade of the twentieth century. In setting aside his brushes and picking up a camera, Magdy had effectively recapitulated, and condensed, the transmedial trajectory of advanced art making that occupied the twentieth century and reimagined it for the twenty-first. Voyaging into this new territory, he nevertheless would carry with him vestiges of past forms, both painterly and cinematic.

THE MUMMY COMPLEX

In his classic 1945 essay "The Ontology of the Photographic Image," the French film theorist André Bazin claimed that if the plastic arts were ever subjected to psychoanalysis, "the practice of embalming the dead might turn out to be a fundamental factor in their creation."[7] This led to an almost inevitable invocation of the ritual burial practices of ancient Egypt and to what Bazin would dub the "mummy complex" as a key underlying factor in figurative art: the preservation of objects against the exigencies of time. While painting and sculpture were dependent upon the vagaries of the artist's eye and hand in this process of mummification, the camera arts, in Bazin's view, represented a significant advance. Technology had come to instrumentalize the fundamental role of representation. This would form the basis of Bazin's influential realist theory of cinema and his remarkably contemporary claim that while "all the arts are based on the presence of man, only photography derives an advantage from his absence."[8]

In Bazin's historical model, the invention of photography effectively freed painting from the burden of representation, a paradigm shift that was deepened by the emergence of the moving image. Yet embedded within painting's past there always were incipient proto-cinematic possibilities. Bazin himself recognized the revolutionary impact of Leonardo da Vinci's use of the camera obscura, while the Soviet filmmaker and theorist Sergei Eisenstein was critically engaged throughout his career with paintings by da Vinci and El Greco.[9] In the same vein, the art historian and early French film theorist Elie Faure produced cinematic readings of Tintoretto's art, while philosopher Jean Paul Sartre, Bazin's contemporary, boldly asserted that Tintoretto was "the first film director."[10] Bazin proved to be no stranger to such comparisons, and in an early discussion of the artistic achievements of Soviet cinema, he hailed Eisenstein as "her Tintoretto."[11]

ARTISTS' CINEMA

By the time the moving image celebrated its centennial in 1995, the relationship between the fine arts and cinema was undergoing a radical reorientation. Through a series of major international exhibitions, in particular the Centre Pompidou's landmark 1989 *Passages de l'image* and *Documenta IX* in Kassel, Germany, in 1992, the longstanding hierarchical relationship that had segregated the camera arts from other practices—dismissing them as mere documentation or (worse) entertainment—was nearing its end. Like the origins of the medium itself, this aesthetic realignment involved technological innovation: the development of high-quality digital projection, the advent of the DVD format, and the emergence of the Internet. As media art historian Erika Balsom has observed, "[W]ithin the sphere of contemporary art, a space . . . opened for a kind of moving image practice that would reflect on the historical institution of cinema, interrogate its present condition, and possibly open pathways into the future."[12] It was a moment that engendered what might be defined as a new form of alternative filmmaking, one that liberated the medium from the dark space of the theater and placed it in the gallery adjacent to painting and sculpture, where it sought its formal parameters somewhere between the experimental cinema and the art film—"a cinema of the museum to be made by artists."[13]

Historically, this period coincided with the building of large museums, galleries, and Kunsthalles dedicated to contemporary art, beginning with the Guggenheim's satellite museum that opened in 1997 in Bilbao, Spain. With larger spaces to fill, curators turned in part to scalable, artist-made moving-image work to meet this need. Many of these artists in turn began to professionalize their production process, which at times approached the scale of independent feature filmmaking, with crews, performers, and production budgets to match. In stark contrast to the economics of the avant-garde cinema and experimental video that had persisted largely outside the museum in previous decades, these new projects were offered as limited editions instead of being available for rental or produced in relatively inexpensive unlimited editions. Artists were becoming film directors for their own gallery-based projects, and a few (most notably the British-born Steve McQueen, Belgian artist Nicolas Provost, and the American Jem Cohen) were able to cross over into feature filmmaking.

THE EYE/I

Basim Magdy's filmmaking practice has unfolded largely at variance with the direction taken by many of his twenty-first century peers. Instead of working with a crew on large-scale productions, he has embraced a semi-artisanal mode that can trace its roots back to the earliest experimental films made by artists such as Marcel Duchamp, Hans Richter, Fernand Léger, and Man Ray in the 1920s. The postwar avant-garde cinema of the 1950s and 60s was equally fueled by art-centric, anti-commercial interventions, as exemplified in the American filmmaker Stan Brakhage's prolific practice and expansive writings. It was Brakhage who advocated "deliberately spitting on the lens or wrecking its focal intention, . . . over-or-under-expos[ing] the film, . . . us[ing] the filters of the world—fog, downpours, unbalanced lights, neons with neurotic color temperatures."[14] These iconoclastic strategies reflect sentiments shared by Magdy, and they are actual techniques he has deployed in producing his own moving-image projects.

Such insurrectionist attitudes have guided much of Magdy's work as he embraced a form of direct intervention onto his celluloid materials by "pickling" his films with a mixture of chemical agents—including such household products as vinegar, rubbing alcohol, and carbonated beverages, some of which are associated, as one of his slide projection titles acknowledges, with "Tear Gas Remedies." He perfected his techniques by trial and error, initially working with Super 8mm film (his first three cartridges were all out of focus) and 35mm color slides. Carefully working with a trio of variables—the type of film stock, the duration of dipping the celluloid into the chemicals, and the particular mix of his pickling agents—Magdy has managed to radically alter the filmstrip just prior to its processing by the lab. The resulting films exhibit striking metallic patinas and tactile surfaces as part of the photochemical transformations the artist has wrought through his aesthetic interventions.

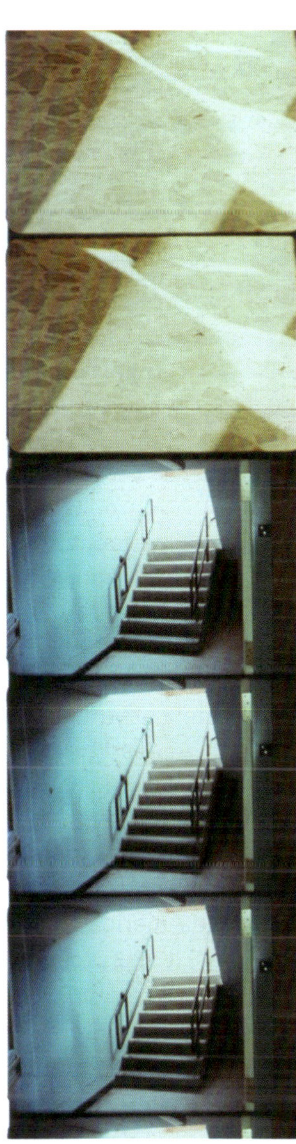

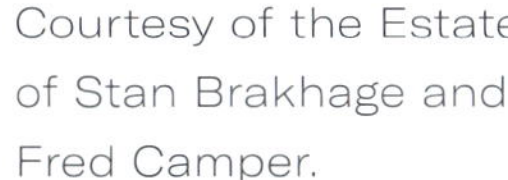
Courtesy of the Estate
of Stan Brakhage and
Fred Camper.

For Brakhage and a generation of his acolytes, these formal alter-ations—breaks with the norms of shooting, direct manipulation of the filmstrip, nonstandard forms of editing—reflected back onto the affective states of the artist. In a particularly provocative formulation, Brakhage claimed: "I am the most thorough documentary film maker in the world because I document the act of seeing as well as everything that the light brings me."[15] This singular perspective was encapsulated in a figure that announced the entwined components of this aesthetic gambit; Brakhage referred to it as the "Eye/I." Such psychologically oriented modes of interpretation recall the era of Action Painting, when the gestural brushwork or trajectories of dripped or poured paint were said to be invested with emotive valences. Madgy's material Interventions never summon up such readings, but reside instead within a cooler, more conceptual register—a marker of its twenty-first-century provenance.

For Magdy, the filming itself often proceeds without any script. As he has noted, "I don't make a storyboard prior to shooting." He tends instead to work in an almost diaristic manner: "I usually take my 16mm camera everywhere I travel and sometimes even on most of my daily outings." He shoots his footage "without knowing what I would eventually use it for, but by now I know myself enough to understand what I may use and what is not important to record."[16] As curator Lauren Cornell describes the resulting footage in discussing *The Dent* (2014), his film work "shares motifs with Magdy's drawings: shots of construction sites, soldiers, and animals recur alongside images of unmarked monuments, aerial shots from planes, lush fields."[17] Regine Basha expands the shot list to include "archaeological ruins, provisionally built environments, bio-domes, surveillance cameras, satellite dishes, and historical monuments."[18] While this lexicon of visual motifs may appear to have been drawn from an archive of stock images, it actually has been created by the artist.

Magdy shares with the Brakhagean cinema an embrace of determinately analogue means, an array of nonstandard methods for producing and assembling his film footage, and a poetic sensibility. For Magdy this often involves the literal use of poetic texts as subtitles and, on occasion, voice-over readings. These texts have been gathered from an array of sources, including the artist's own poetic writings and sometimes the writings of his father, artist Magdy El-Gohary, as well as from historical accounts and what he has termed "sheer absurdity." Unlike Brakhage, who made resolutely silent films, Magdy creates his own scores using original compositions and musical downloads that are often, like his imagery, subjected to distorting procedures (stretching and reversal). The resulting soundtracks, like their textual counterparts, do not necessarily "line up."[19] Each of the individual channels—the book space of reading, the sonic intervention into the silent image, and the color-altered camera rolls—maintains more than its measure of independence.

Despite these independently operating strands of image, sound, and text, Magdy's films are nonetheless imbued with structural coherence through the traces of certain formal features and established viewing protocols that undergird the whole. Three key genres of the filmic avant-garde, for instance, appear periodically in Magdy's films: portraiture, landscape, and diary.[20] There equally are proto-narrative elements (characters, locales, actions) and an interplay among image, music, and text that activate a search for patterns of repetition and resolution as well as dramatic trajectories, which nonetheless never materialize.[21]

At other times his films—for example, *The Dent* and *The Everyday Ritual of Solitude Hatching Monkeys* (2014)—operate like art films, or what the literary critic Norman Holland called "puzzling movies." As he observed about this historical form of European filmmaking, "They puzzle us as to their meaning in a total sense. They puzzle us scene-by-scene simply as to what is going on in a narrative or dramatic way."[22] Film historian David Bordwell has traced the source of this dilemma to the art film's use of characters who "lack defined desires and goals," which creates a "drifting episodic quality." Especially useful in describing Magdy's films is what he terms a "broken teleology . . . in which events become pared down toward a picaresque successivity."[23] Therein resides both the sense of puzzlement and the absurdist humor one experiences in encountering Magdy's cinematic tales. In mining the experimental strategies of the film avant-garde and the disjointed narrative ambience of classic art films, and overlaying these with a sampling of textural and sonic elements, Magdy creates multidimensional works that define a new "other" cinema—a rapprochement of old and new, visual and textual, aural and cerebral.

One subtitle in *The Dent*, appended to imagery shot from an airplane window, informs us that "Everyone partied and no one cared." Then, in a static image of a gravestone adorned with a floral bouquet, we learn more: "They ate the meat then stuffed the carcasses." While Magdy never fully identifies who "they" are, we nevertheless may feel that we have encountered them before. The German philosopher Martin Heidegger, for example, devoted several key passages of his landmark treatise *Being and Time* (1927) to what he calls "the 'they'" (das Man). This conceptual entity is at the core of the public sphere, though Heidegger warns us that their identity is elusive: "not this one, not that one, not oneself, not some people, and not the sum of them all."[24] *The Dent*, with its narrative that revolves around a case study of civic delusion—an unnamed town aspires to serve as the host city for the Olympics—allegorizes the consequences of this Heideggerian quandary of the individual at sea in a world systematically informed by the beliefs and attitudes to which "they" adhere.

While the traditional medium for philosophical discourse remains language, in Magdy's films there is a marked tendency to engage in what aesthetician and film historian Noël Carroll describes as the practice of "movies making philosophy."[25] Part of this can be sensed in the manner in which the artist problematizes the viewing experience by purposely failing to align his images with his texts and music. Language never serves as captions, images never serve as illustrations, and the scores for his films function much like the music that accompanies Merce Cunningham's dances, which operate on distinct parallel tracks rather than defining interpretive registers. Magdy's films use what Carroll terms "phenomenological address," not only to encourage viewers to adopt an apperceptive (meta-perceptual) position in deciphering the deployment of proto-narrative elements, but also to advance philosophical insights gleaned from the artist's own observations of the human condition.[26]

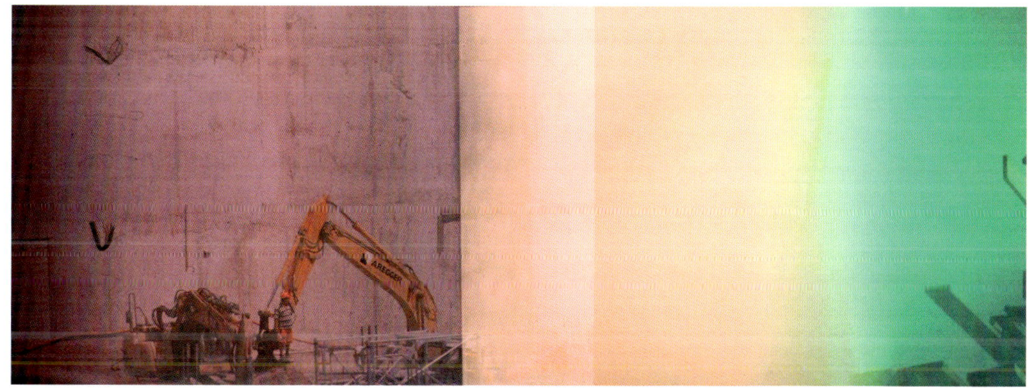

Basim Magdy, *A 240 Second Analysis of Failure and Hopefulness (With Coke, Vinegar and Other Tear Gas Remedies)*, 2012.

The most explicit example of this latter philosophical mode can be experienced in Magdy's *13 Essential Rules for Understanding the World* (2011), a short digitally projected work with a didactic title that traffics in mock-serious instructional film voice-overs, or what Omar Kholeif has aptly described as an "existential journey through the looking glass of life."[27] Despite its digital display, the film opens with the sound of old-fashioned film-projector clatter, which effectively sets the scene for imagery originally captured on the resolutely amateur Super 8mm format. Here, the digital present meets the analogue past on common ground. Complementing the home-movie ambience of the Super 8 gauge is an array of childlike imagery, which initially seems at variance with many of Magdy's other films. The visuals consist of handheld close-ups of red or yellow tulips, their petals decorated with crude faces drawn on with felt-tip markers. As the title suggests, the work is divided into thirteen sections, each of which focuses on one of the titled "rules," presented simultaneously in matched voice-over and subtitles. Interspersed between the still lifes of tulips is a set of images that loosely maintain childhood associations: an extreme long shot of a bunch of red balloons floating skyward, a young woman balancing atop a boulder on one foot, other young women riding under a bridge on horseback, an archaic iris-framed long shot of a carnival ride, a close-up of a wooden toy swinging on a string.

The rules themselves include what Regine Basha describes as sensible, Dharma-like lessons, such as "2. Never try to change anything. You can't even change yourself."[28] Others involve more politically engaged propositions, reminiscent of American artist Jenny Holzer's *Truisms*, as in "5. Never fall under the false spell of doing good with money. If money didn't exist in the first place, neither would the poor." Adding a certain poignancy to this series of mainly dispiriting maxims, Magdy employs cello samples downloaded from the Internet and stretched into ominous registers. Together, language and music counter the seeming casualness of the image track, producing in the process (to paraphrase the title of a composition by Benjamin Britten) a "Young Person's Guide to Existential Philosophy."

THE ANGEL OF HISTORY

In the critical literature on Magdy, Walter Benjamin's Angel of History makes a brief appearance.[29] His film *The Many Colors of the Sky Radiate Forgetfulness* (2014) thematizes the issue of cultural memory through its juxtaposition of a bestiary of taxidermied animals—a literalization of Bazin's notion of the "mummy complex"—with texts that question the viability of such animate carriers of the past. The experience of living beings is fleeting on this earth; historical consciousness can only be contained in the traces of material things, as the film informs us: "Only stone, bronze and the sky shall outlive all the rest." At a meta-level, Magdy seems to suggest that analogue film itself may have a role to play in this eschatological archive, given its capacity to capture and contain the disparate artifacts that continually attract the artist's attention—demolition sites and architectural ruins, off-season fairgrounds and art storage facilities, fossils and carved-out landforms. Like Benjamin's Angel of History, Magdy's media-based work maintains a steady gaze upon the past as it flows forward into the future, carrying along discontinuous fragments of the visible evidence of our cultural pasts—deposited within the grain of the emulsion, residing atop its denatured celluloid skin, locked into the chemistry of its C-prints.

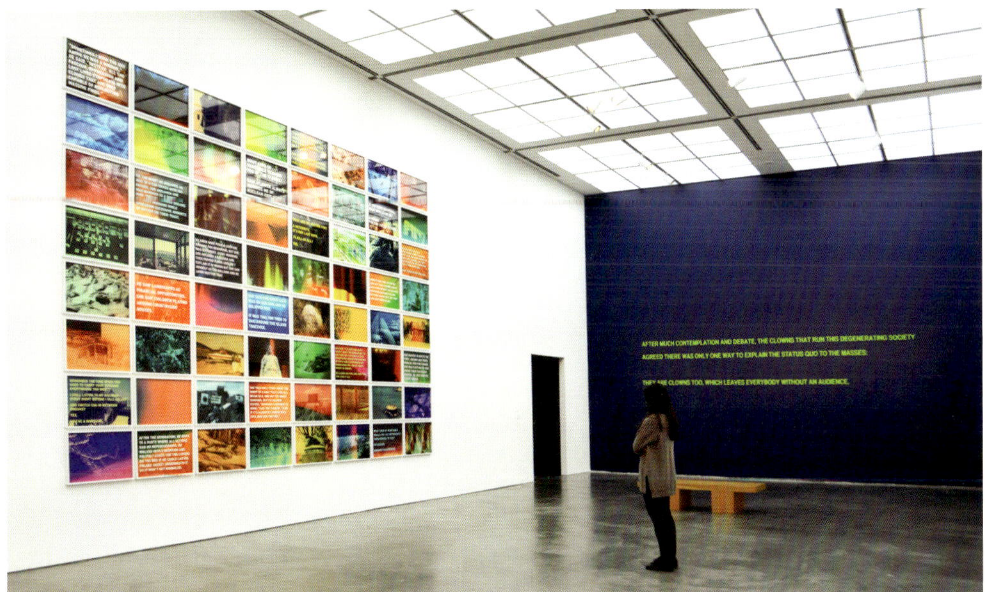

Installation view of *Basim Magdy: The Stars Were Aligned for a Century of New Beginnings*, Museum of Contemporary Art, Chicago, 2016–2017.

In the end, Basim Magdy's art prepares us for a complex world in which the past is a contested realm that may be retrievable only through mustering outmoded machine-age technology, photochemical materials, and dystopic narratives as shields against the constant onslaught of frictionless forms of streaming media and the "*über*-archive of the database." By deinstrumentalizing the digital, parsing and complicating the separate channels of image, text, and music, and deaccelerating the production of meaning, Magdy's art is already a model through which we can envision a distinctly twenty-first–century art of resistance.

Bruce Jenkins is Professor of Film, Video, New Media, and Animation at the School of the Art Institute of Chicago. He has authored a book on Gordon Matta-Clark for Afterall and edited a volume of writings by Hollis Frampton for the MIT Press. His writings have appeared in *Aperture*, *Artforum*, *Millennium Film Journal*, and *Mousse*, as well as in exhibition catalogues for the Guggenheim Museum, Museum of Contemporary Art (Los Angeles), Renaissance Society, Tate Modern, Wexner Center, and Whitney Museum. He co-authored the forthcoming catalogue raisonné of the films of Andy Warhol, volume 2.

ENDNOTES

1 See "Introduction," *October*, no. 100, special issue "Obsolescence" (Spring 2002): 3–5.

2 Walter Benjamin, *Illuminations*, ed. Hannah Arendt, trans. Harry Zohn (New York: Schocken Books, 1973), 258.

3 "Introduction," *October*, no. 100: 4, 5.

4 Basim Magdy, classroom lecture delivered at the School of the Art Institute of Chicago (SAIC), October 31, 2018.

5 Bart Simpson makes a brief reappearance more than a decade later in Magdy's film *No Shooting Stars* (2016), in a subtitled passage in which the textual protagonist states: "I am the two-dimensional evil twinkle in Bart Simpson's eyes as he hears the words "the land that law forgot."

6 On the proto-cinematic aspects of Magdy's early paintings and drawings, see Regine Basha, "Accounts of Human Bureaucracy: The Elusive Narrative in the Work of Basim Magdy," in *Basim Magdy: Would a Firefly Fear the Fire that Burns in Its Heart?*, exh. cat. (Berlin: Deutsche Bank; Ostfildern: Hatje Cantz, 2016), 135.

7 André Bazin, "The Ontology of the Photographic Image," in *What Is Cinema?*, ed. and trans. Hugh Gray (Berkeley: University of California Press, 1971), 9.

8 Ibid., 13.

9 See Bazin, "The Ontology of the Photographic Image," 11; on Eisenstein's fascination with da Vinci and El Greco, see Gilles Deleuze, *Cinema 2: The Time-Image*, trans. Hugh Tomlinson and Robert Galeta (Minneapolis: University of Minnesota Press, 1989), 156.

10 Peter Schjeldahl, "All In: The Vicarious Thrill of Tintoretto," *New Yorker*, April 1, 2019, 76.

11 Bazin, "The Ontology of the Photographic Image," 12n.

12 Erika Balsom, *Exhibiting Cinema in Contemporary Art* (Amsterdam: Amsterdam University Press, 2013), 37.

13 Ibid., 38.

14 Stan Brakhage, "Metaphors on Vision," *Film Culture*, no. 30 (Fall 1963): n.p.

15 Stan Brakhage, quoted in Hollis Frampton, "Stan and Jane Brakhage Talking," *Artforum* 11, no. 5 (January 1973): 79.

16 Basim Magdy, email correspondence with the author, February 19, 2018.

17 Lauren Cornell, "A Grave for Utopia," in *Basim Magdy: Would a Firefly Fear the Fire that Burns in Its Heart?*, 24.

18 Basha, "Accounts of Human Bureaucracy," 136.

19 Ibid., 138.

20 On these generic forms, see "Afterword (1997): Lee Russell Interviews Peter Wollen," in Peter Wollen, *Signs and Meaning in the Cinema*, 5th ed. (London: British Film Institute, 2013), 235.

21 As Omar Kholeif has observed about Magdy's filmmaking, "[A]lthough often seemingly linear in its construction, [it] is rarely driven by a storyline." See Omar Kholeif, "Shimmering World—In and Around the Work of Basim Magdy," in *Basim Magdy: Would a Firefly Fear the Fire that Burns in Its Heart?*, 85.

22 Norman N. Holland, *The Dynamics of Literary Response* (New York: W. W. Norton, 1975), 164.

23 David Bordwell, "The Art Cinema as a Mode of Film Practice," in *The European Cinema Reader*, ed. Catherine Fowler (London: Routledge, 2002), 96.

24 Martin Heidegger, *Being and Time*, trans. John Macquarrie and Edward Robinson (New York: Harper and Row, 1962), 164.
25 Noël Carroll, *Minerva's Night Out: Philosophy, Pop Culture, and Moving Pictures* (Chichester, West Sussex: Wiley-Blackwell, 2013), 204.
26 Ibid., 207, where Carroll introduces the concept of "phenomenological address."
27 Kholeif, "Shimmering World," 89.
28 Basha, "Accounts of Human Bureaucracy," 140.
29 Regina Basha suggested this allusion to Benjamin's Angel of History in her analysis of the pickled images in Magdy's *The Many Colors of the Sky Radiate Forgetfulness*. See Basha, "Accounts of Human Bureaucracy," 140–41.

KENDRA PAITZ We're going to talk about your use of film, but your writing is what initially drew me to your work. It was when I saw *The Dent* (2014) in *Surround Audience*, the 2015 triennial at the New Museum in New York City. I was captivated by your poetic style, in which there are many open-ended possibilities, and how you negotiate between fantasy and reality, history and the future. You've talked about being a "failed poet" as a teenager, but you said that working with film offered you a way to tap into that sensibility.

BASIM MAGDY I love writing, but it took me years to realize that my interest in words comes from a desire to make sense of mostly fragmented and unrelated ideas in a language that's intelligible. After I filmed some footage for *The Dent*, I started writing a fictional narrative where one story stems out of another. They run parallel to one another and meet in the end. I wanted to make a film about collective failure and aspiration: a realistic form of hopefulness. The film is also about generations and the cycles of revolt and "make believe" they go through. Every generation believes it can accomplish what the ones before couldn't. We're all blinded by the peculiarities of the times we live in. I wanted to squeeze all of this into a subtly humorous and fictional narrative that doesn't say any of this in a literal way, a narrative that leaves room for imagination and different responses. *The Dent* was the first film where I felt that I reached a harmonious balance between image, sound, and a poetically scripted narrative. I realized that poetry doesn't have to be just words, but a composition of these three elements. At the same time, I don't believe any of these elements could survive on their own. Their dependence on one another helped give the film meaning.

KP You were originally trained as a painter. Could you talk about that background?

BM My father, Magdy El-Gohary, is an artist and throughout my childhood, he painted, made delicate watercolors, and created the most intricate botanical illustrations for scientific books. He also continues to write short stories. My mother is a retired architect. Growing up in a family surrounded by art and creative thinking helped me enjoy drawing and painting as a child. When I was 14, I decided I would become an artist, which was a very uninformed and premature decision. I went to a very traditional and conservative art school in Cairo where time seemed to stop in the mid-twentieth century. I ended up leading a double life. I would finish the projects that we were assigned in a few days, then travel back to my parents' house to make big, raw, colorful, and aggressive paintings. The silver lining to five wasted years in art school was that experimenting and doing things my way became part of the process of educating myself as an artist. After I graduated, I did a few artist residencies and started showing my paintings. A couple of years later, I felt the need for the elements in the paintings to move and become part of a narrative, so I hired an animator to help me animate my drawings. For the years that followed, I worked with installation, sculpture, filmmaking, text, and photography. Painting always ran parallel to everything else I was doing. It has always been the fastest way to capture ideas.

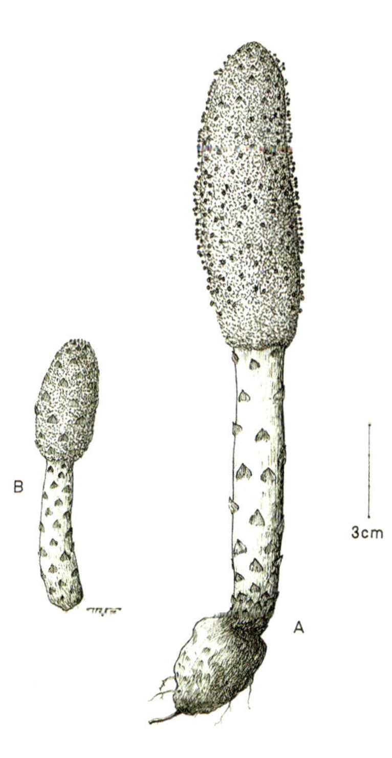
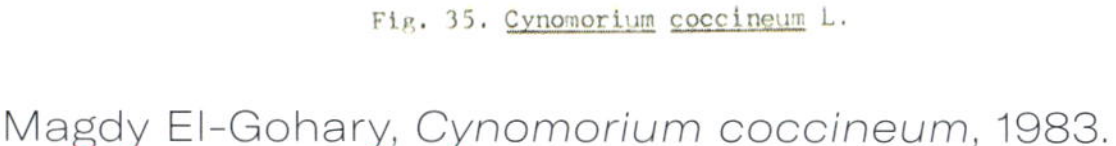

Magdy El-Gohary, *Cynomorium coccineum*, 1983.

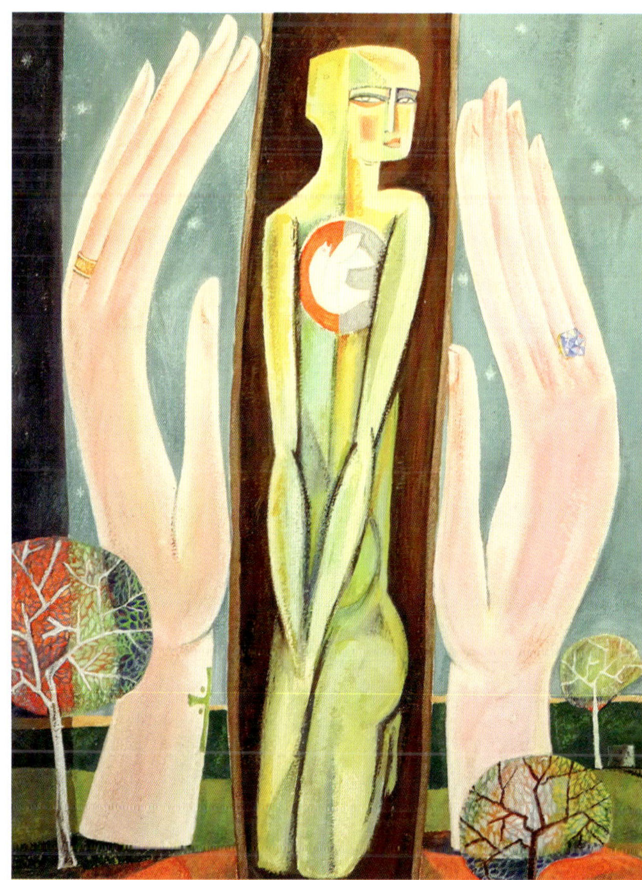

Magdy El-Gohary, *Tenderness*, 1968.

KP What prompted you to start working with film?
The ways you explore its materiality are exciting and often surprising.

BM Film is tactile. I can hold it in my hand and see my fingerprints on it. I can put it in chemicals or impose light leaks on the film itself by opening the camera while it's running. I can punch holes in it. This tactility allows film to be altered in many ways but also makes it precious. At some point, I wanted to make layered work to mirror the linearity of time, to use comprehensible language and sound. I wanted to make fiction about the way I experience the world. Video seemed too nice, too perfect, too real. Film, on the other hand, with its grain and contrast, felt more like painted sequences. As limiting as film can be in financial terms, its layers allow me unmatched freedom and pleasure.

KP You just mentioned the light leaks, but could you talk about the other ways you manipulate the film stock to achieve painterly distortions of image and color for your films and photos?

BM My experience with film started with Super 8 because of its contrast, grain, and indifference to detail, but its tactility was what assured me that images representing the objects of our surroundings—that we perceive as reality—should be tactile too. Whether film, a printed photograph, or a slide projection created through the poetic passing of light through space to create a colorful image on a surface, a representation should be separated from what it represents. I wanted to change the characteristics of film to find new ways of depicting the multi-dimensionality and complexity of reality while maintaining its familiarity. I read a blog where someone put a roll of film in the dishwasher. The results were radiant, colorful, and unpredictable. I tried it myself and the results were less exciting, but I was intrigued. I embarked on understanding the chemistry and sensitivity of film. I collected different film stocks and spent two months in my pitch-dark bathroom dipping the film in a variety of acidic and alkaline household chemicals before getting it processed by the lab. Eventually I put together tables detailing the reactions between every film stock, chemical, duration of exposure, and result. If you take ten different kinds of film stock and put them in the same acidic chemical for the same duration, they will all produce different results affecting color dominance, drips, dots, and loss of sharpness. I think of everything I do as fiction, and fiction calls for uncertainty and surrender to a certain degree of randomness.

For the three films I finished in 2014, I used masks inside the camera, pickled the film stock in household chemicals, and shot footage through kaleidoscopes I built myself. Earlier, in 2013, I intentionally filmed *Crystal Ball* with a cracked camera to allow light to leak onto the film while it was rolling. I believe reality is more exciting when partly experienced through the imagination.

> **KP** You told me in our first studio visit that older film stocks like Super 8 and 16mm don't have the same nostalgic quality for you as they do for many people who associate their properties with home movies and family memories.

BM I only discovered Super 8 film in my early 30s. Growing up in Egypt, no one around me had access to a movie camera. The color saturation, high contrast, and lower-than-life quality of the image resonated with me when I shot my first three film cartridges, but what really struck me was the beauty of the grain. It felt like the twin sibling of the hazy spray paint effect I created in my works on paper at the time. More than anything, I find myself intrigued by film in all formats and see an abundance of possibilities to work with in the future.

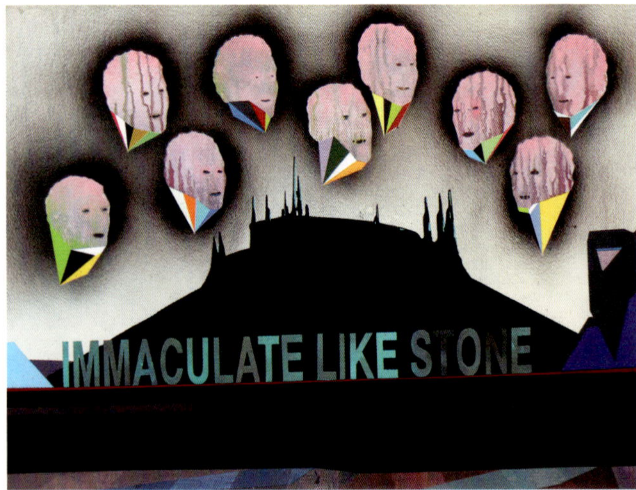

Basim Magdy, *They Shot a Movie with Frozen Butterflies and Cautious Optimism*, 2012.

> **KP** The three components of image, text, and sound in your films are all comprised of what you've filmed, written, and recorded. I think people are often surprised to discover that all the colors are analogue. When I first visited you in Chicago during your Hyde Park Art Center residency, you had grids of stills pinned to the wall so you could determine the sequence of imagery and develop the writing. Do you use this method for all of the films? And where, when, how does the sound come into it?

BM My films always start with what seems like an abundance of unrelated footage that I constantly shoot in different locations as I travel for shows. In the case of *The Dent*, the footage was shot in twelve different cities within a year. The footage gets transferred to video files and I take screenshots of every scene. Those screenshots get printed in a grid and they end up stuck on a movable wall in my studio. Laying everything out in front of me allows me to envision the film as a whole, detached from the linearity of time and the sequences. I start writing in response to the printed screenshots, then I shoot more footage in response to what I wrote. I repeat the process of going back and forth between writing and shooting footage until I'm happy with what I have. The soundtrack is the glue that binds the other two elements together. I'm always listening to what's around me and constantly recording sound either on my phone or a more professional sound recorder. While editing, those field recordings end up getting stretched, reversed, and layered along with a few downloaded samples to become the soundtrack. Eventually the film evolves like a collaged composition. The narrative, sound, and footage keep changing together until I feel the film is ready.

> **KP** Most of your photographic projects begin in a similar way, with you bringing your cameras wherever you go. *Every Subtle Gesture* (2012–2016) is comprised of a collection of travel photos you took in the late 1990s, which you later individually paired with lines of text. The phrases range from mildly (or wildly) dystopian to darkly humorous. The elongated neck of a gray-green sauropod swoops upward into the leaden sky over a low horizon of leafless trees and a few high-rise buildings with text reading, "AND THE ROAD WAS PAVED WITH THE CRUSHED BONES OF OUR LOVED ONES." Or a double exposure—with a light leak or "pickling" leading to a rainbow effect—of ghostly buildings and implements hovering over an otherwise peaceful seascape with text reading, "NATIONS STUTTER AND ENTER INTO ALLIANCES TO WAIL LIKE TRAPPED GHOSTS." Or illuminated globes on display amidst draping crimson velvet curtains with text reading, "METEOROLOGISTS ARGUED IT WAS CAUSED BY A SNEEZING GIANT."

BM *Every Subtle Gesture* started in 2012 when I was asked to do a solo show and, for the first time in my life, had no new ideas. At the time, I was starting to shoot footage for *The Dent*. I was preoccupied with the complexity and fluidity of collective aspiration and failure. I remembered an old box of photographs from my first trip outside Egypt. I had just bought a camera to document what I may not see again. As I was recalling the memories the photographs were meant to capture, I tried to read the photographs in complete detachment from those memories. I started writing unusual interpretations in the form of a line of text under each photograph and continued to do that until 2016. By that point, the series had reached 100 works. This was the beginning of an attempt to create narrative while breaking down its rigid linearity. Works in series that combine images and text make it visually possible to experience different parts of a spread-out narrative at the same time. I did this differently and on a larger scale with *An Apology to a Love Story that Crashed into a Whale* (2016), in which a large-scale photographic grid comprised of 64 prints tells a fictional and fragmented love story through images, events, conversations, and dreams. Nothing about the work is linear or chronological, but it's all there on the wall. I wanted to create a narrative that defies the time-based structure of moving images, but mainly it was the realization of an old desire to make an artwork about love in a way that people can relate to through their own love stories and experiences.

> **KP** *The Everyday Ritual of Solitude Hatching Monkeys* is loosely categorized as part of a trilogy with *The Dent* and *The Many Colors of the Sky Radiate Forgetfulness*, all created in 2014. *The Everyday Ritual…* was inspired by one of your father's stories and relates to your 2017 photographic work *We're All Victims of Our Own Adopted Fantasies Here (reprise)*. How did one action in the film lead to these five photographs?

BM Because all three films were finished in 2014, they ended up feeling related in many ways. With *The Dent*, I had finally found a formula for interweaving narrative, moving image, and a layered soundtrack where they mostly hint to one another and are rarely synced in a traditional sense. I became interested in the space left for imagination and personal associations created by this way of composing films. *The Dent* was about the absurd undertones of collective aspiration. In *The Many Colors of the Sky Radiate Forgetfulness* I tried to explore the fading of collective memory, and in *The Everyday Ritual of Solitude Hatching Monkeys*, I turned to my father's short stories, which I had first read as a teenager. I adapted a narrative from a few of them about a man who feels alienated by his own society, so he moves away and adopts a new one, only to have its members flee to the beach as soon as he arrives. He sits alone in his office, staring at the coffee patterns in his cup. Eventually he picks up the phone and dials a random number. An absurdly romantic conversation ensues between him and the woman who picks up, one that's full of longing for someone he's never met. I wanted to elaborate on this conversation by creating another work that explores its ambiguity, but I didn't want to explain it. Making *We're All Victims of Our Own Adopted Fantasies Here (reprise)* was an attempt to give the phone conversation an octopus tentacle with its own independent mind. I tried to imagine the visual image the fictional protagonist constructed of someone he's never met: the fantasy. It ended up being a colorful, fragmented, and dense photographic work. To me it's like a reprise in a musical composition, a tune repeated elsewhere to have a life of its own.

> **KP** You've also been writing for large-scale text-based murals, beginning with *Clowns* (2014) with florescent yellow-green text on a blue or black wall, and growing with *Eternity* (2018), again text on a painted wall, which you created for our exhibition. For *Eternity*, the wall was a radiant gradient of goldenrod to magenta paint, with white bars and vibrant blue lettering. You said it should read like a poem and that its inspiration began when you were recently visiting an archaeological site.

BM I like to think of *Eternity* as a visual poem, a poem that is to be seen and read at the same time. I was visiting the funerary complex of King Djoser in Saqqara, Egypt, and although it is mostly known for Djoser's Step Pyramid, the first of all the ancient Egyptian Pyramids, there are many other scattered tombs (and a few other pyramids too). I thought about death and all the generations that have lived and died before us, all the individually significant lives that were deemed collectively insignificant, all the memories that history chose to forget.

Eternity is fragmented and definitely not about Djoser or his pyramid. It's about fate, distance, the randomness of events, and the shape of time. "I'm in Union Square about to get on the train" was part of a phone conversation I had with a friend. I found myself transported to that place. I could visualize my friend's words. It was important to include this line to maintain a connection to reality. Lives start resembling giant soap bubbles floating in the air above sidewalks as kids jump around them in excitement. They're constantly changing shape, size, and rainbow colors. I was reading about the shape of time—a cone, a corkscrew—and I wanted people to relate to it, not just scientifically. The gradient could be a sunset or a sunrise, this is how we know time exists, it passes. Not everything has to make sense, not in art and definitely not in life.

> **KP** Your work is often cited as dystopian—and there are certainly elements of that—but you also embrace fun and experimentation in your participatory projects like the game, *PINGPINPOOLPONG, or How I Learned to Laugh at Failure* (2018) and #dearbasim (2017–present) on Instagram.* These are fairly democratic pursuits, much like your decision to make your films accessible online in their entirety. What prompted these decisions?

BM I remember thinking that no one would take *13 Essential Rules for Understanding the World* (2011) seriously. It wasn't included in any shows for two years after I made it, but I had put it on my website during this period. Most people thought this was a miscalculated move. Some thought films by artists should only be viewed in art settings. Others worried about copyright and how this might affect future sales of the film. I was making films for people to watch, and putting my films online seemed like the obvious way for this to happen. During those two years, someone posted a couple of screenshots from the film on a popular Tumblr account.

People from different parts of the world re-blogged them and watched the film. As an artist who makes films, you can either show them in art exhibitions or, if you're lucky enough, at film festivals too. In both cases you are limited by geography. The sad reality is that because exhibitions and festival productions require big budgets, in 90% of the cases, I end up showing my work physically in First World countries. I have no interest in limiting the visibility of my work to First World audiences. It's a matter of principle for me. Putting my films online is an attempt to make the films accessible and to start random and unexpected discussions about them. With the Instagram hashtag #dearbasim, I tried to extend the same desire to communicate to exhibition visitors whom I may never meet. I always wondered what happens to a show after its opening: what people look at, what attracts their attention, what my work makes them think of. I created a platform that eventually became an archive of some of those thoughts, feelings, and responses. To take it a step further, I ask people to change or manipulate the work as a means of collaboration.

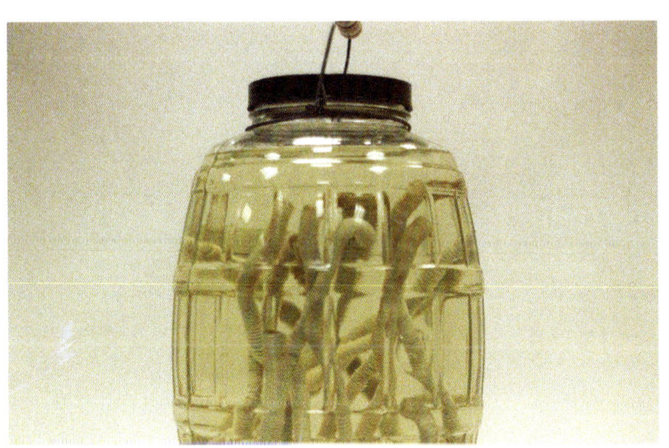
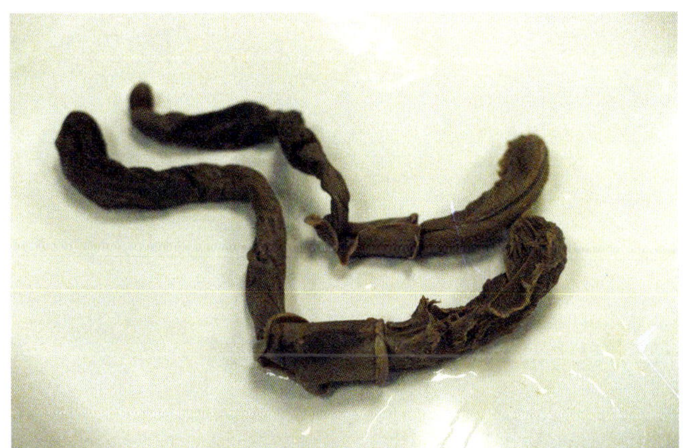

Preserved giant tube worm specimens at the Collections Resource Center of the Field Museum, Chicago, photographed by Basim Magdy.

KP Several people responded to *No Shooting Stars* (2016) for #dearbasim during our exhibition. When I was leading tours, visitors seemed to connect with the film's sense of mystery and discovery relating to the ocean. Sometimes we would exchange stories or examples, and I would often share that I had recently read about the discovery of a species of shark near an active underwater volcano, even though the heat and acidity seemed like they would preclude the survival of life such as that.

BM For *No Shooting Stars*, I started with the fact that there have been more trips to the moon than to certain depths of the ocean. I watched a lot of documentaries about how little we know about those depths and their inhabitants. A lot of my research focused on underwater black smokers and the giant tube worms that latch to their edges. Because those creatures live under crushing water pressure, in complete darkness and unusual temperatures, surrounded by methane and highly toxic hydrogen sulfide, their discovery changed the way astronomers anticipate life on other planets. The ocean showed us that life could exist under unexpected conditions. Towards the end of my residency in Chicago, I visited the storage of the Field Museum. I asked if they had giant tube worm specimens and it turned out they are one of very few museums that have them. Holding a specimen in my hand, even if devoid of color and life, was a very emotional moment. It was as if something impossible and almost fictional had just come to life through its very demise. After all, the biggest advantage those creatures have is that humans can't reach them.

In the end, I opted for making a more poetic and ambiguous film with fragments of human perception of the ocean throughout the past, present, and a projected future, where mythology, lost civilizations, box jellyfish, island high-security prisons, nuclear leaks, disfigured mermaids, and underwater Internet cables coexist in a fictional narrative. I wanted the film to be about the uncertainty, the surprises, and the lack of knowledge. I wanted it to be about the ocean being much bigger and more mysterious than we can ever comprehend. That if ever asked about what it thinks of life on land, the ocean wouldn't even care to respond.

KP *No Shooting Stars* was the most recent film at the time of our exhibition, but you have just completed two new ones: *M . A . G . N . E . T* and *New Acid*, both in 2019. There have been seismic shifts in terms of global politics and awareness of environmental issues since completion of *No Shooting Stars*. I know you're not interested in making didactic works, but did you notice a deeper leaning in your tendencies toward or away from the fictional for these two films, or in your desire to incorporate any new techniques?

BM I finished *New Acid* and *M . A . G . N . E . T* less than four months apart, but it was essential for me that they would end up completely different from each other. They started as two independent ideas. As they grew simultaneously over the last year, and particularly in their final stages, they drifted even more apart. Despite that, in both films I continued to explore new ways—to me—of exploring fiction, the absurd, and humor while attempting to swiftly glide between the past, present, and an imagined future. In *New Acid*, several animals chat via text messages. Between their mundane exchanges of words void of life, conflict and rivalry emerge. Their mirrored physical appearance hints to entrapment inside a reality-T.V. show, one where uncertainty and doubt prevail. Social media-induced insecurities and escapism become evidence that at least some of them are not bots. They question selfishness, self-love, and self-destruction. They question the role of tradition in growing racism. They propose nostalgia and nationalism as identical twins. And as the reality about their entrapment inside a zoo unfolds, visitors nicknamed "the ugly ones" arrive wearing their "cheesy sunglasses." One of the first things that intrigued me about the geography of zoos is that most animal species don't know of the existence of the other animals in the same zoo. The only thing that connects them is the gaze of the human visitors and their phone cameras. There is something extremely sad and poetic about the restrictions on communication in a situation like this.

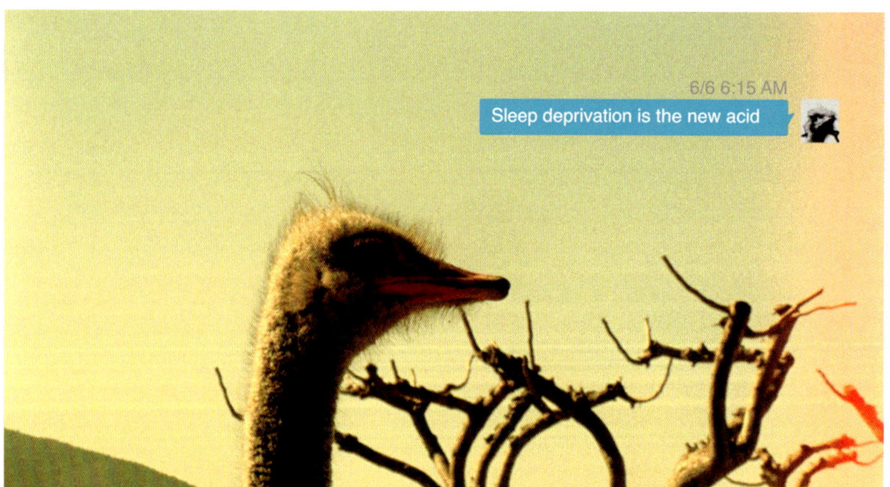

Basim Magdy, *New Acid*, 2019.

M . A . G . N . E . T starts with a helium-filled balloon floating in the sky above Manhattan, a year before the fictional discovery that Earth's gravity is increasing, and ends with the collapse of the stock market in New York. In between, human history is re-evaluated, and new truths arise about our forgotten past. This film is very colorful; almost every scene was shot with a different combination of color filters. Even in the most apocalyptic scenarios, colorful hope is the seed for new ways of thinking and understanding.

> *Basim Magdy invites audience members to take their own snapshots or videos of his work, with which they can create a parody, make an alteration, or offer commentary. These are then shared on Instagram with #dearbasim, and the artist responds to the participants online. Follow #dearbasim on Instagram to see the range of responses created since 2017. Several meaningful interactions were generated via #dearbasim during the exhibition at University Galleries, including one about someone's childhood dream of becoming the first female astronaut. Another facilitated hilarious and candid interactions between the artist and several young children participating in one of our educational workshops.

Kendra Paitz is Director and Chief Curator at University Galleries of Illinois State University. She has organized solo exhibitions and edited accompanying monographs for Terry Adkins, Stephanie Brooks, Kendell Carter, Juan Angel Chávez, Bethany Collins, Oliver Herring, Basim Magdy, Melanie Schiff, and Carrie Schneider, among others. Her group exhibitions include *An Infinite and Omnivorous Sky, Strange Oscillations and Vibrations of Sympathy*, and *The House of the Seven Gables*.

27

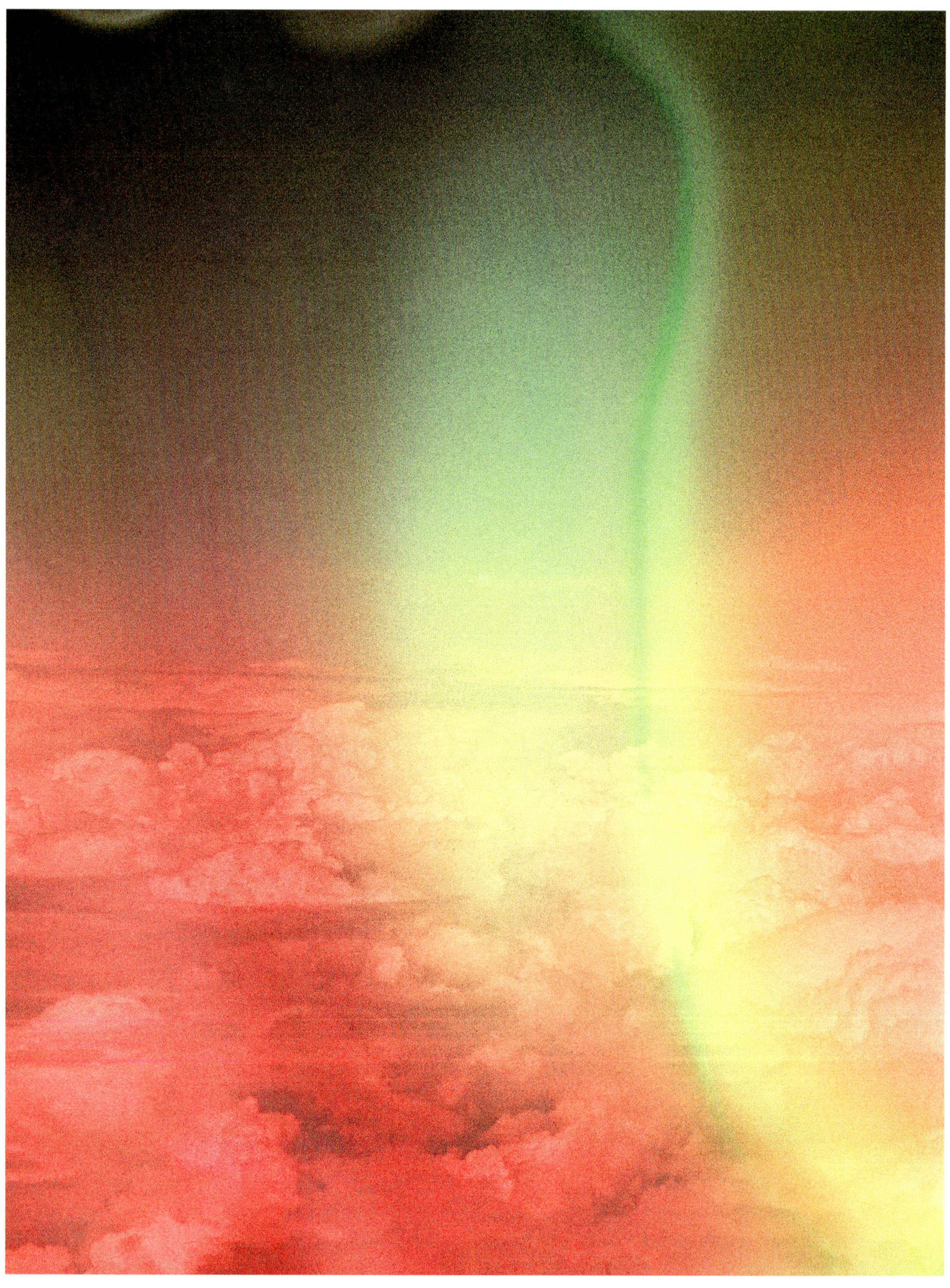

6. NEVER LET YOURSELF FALL ASLEEP.

YOU'LL DREAM.

7. NEVER TRY TO MAKE A POINT.

NO ONE WILL EVER CARE.

An excerpt from the script of *13 Essential Rules for Understanding the World*, 2011.

13 ESSENTIAL RULES FOR UNDERSTANDING THE WORLD

2011

SUPER 8 FILM TRANSFERRED
TO FULL HD VIDEO.

5:16 MINUTES

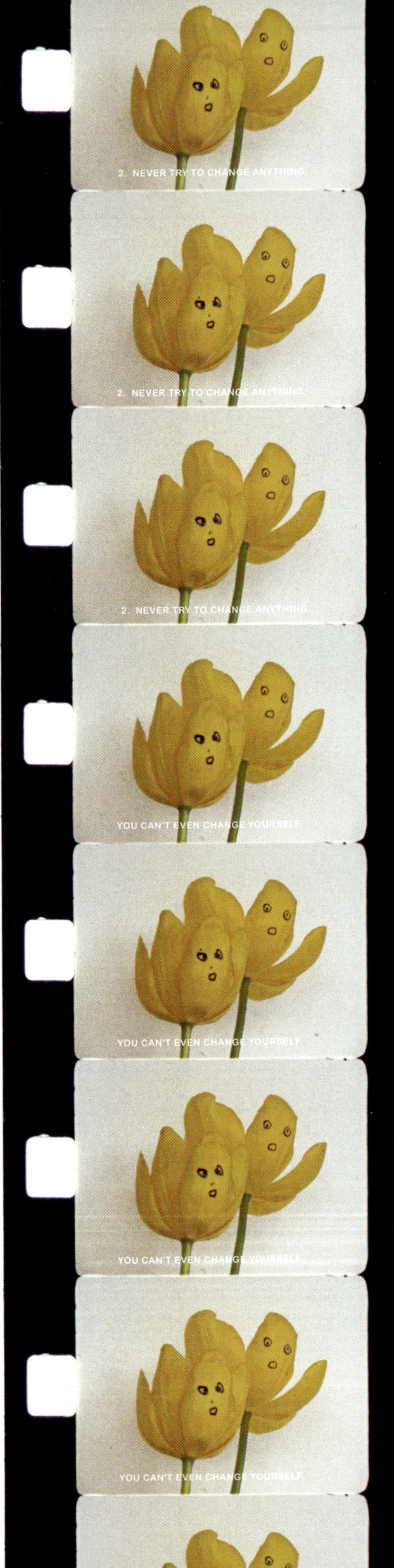

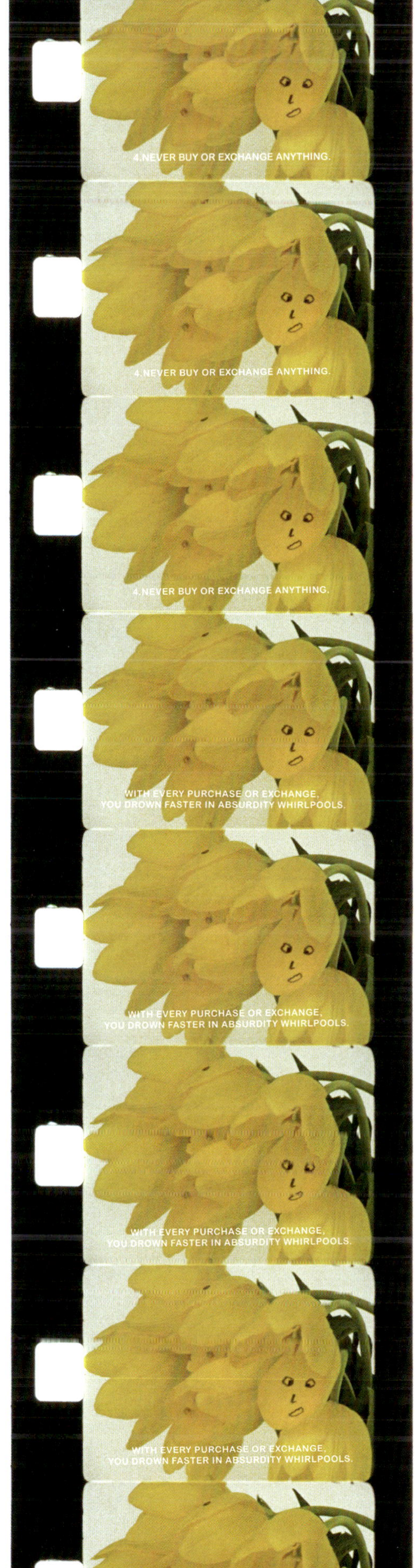
4.NEVER BUY OR EXCHANGE ANYTHING.
4.NEVER BUY OR EXCHANGE ANYTHING.
4.NEVER BUY OR EXCHANGE ANYTHING.
WITH EVERY PURCHASE OR EXCHANGE,
YOU DROWN FASTER IN ABSURDITY WHIRLPOOLS.
WITH EVERY PURCHASE OR EXCHANGE,
YOU DROWN FASTER IN ABSURDITY WHIRLPOOLS.
WITH EVERY PURCHASE OR EXCHANGE,
YOU DROWN FASTER IN ABSURDITY WHIRLPOOLS.
WITH EVERY PURCHASE OR EXCHANGE,
YOU DROWN FASTER IN ABSURDITY WHIRLPOOLS.

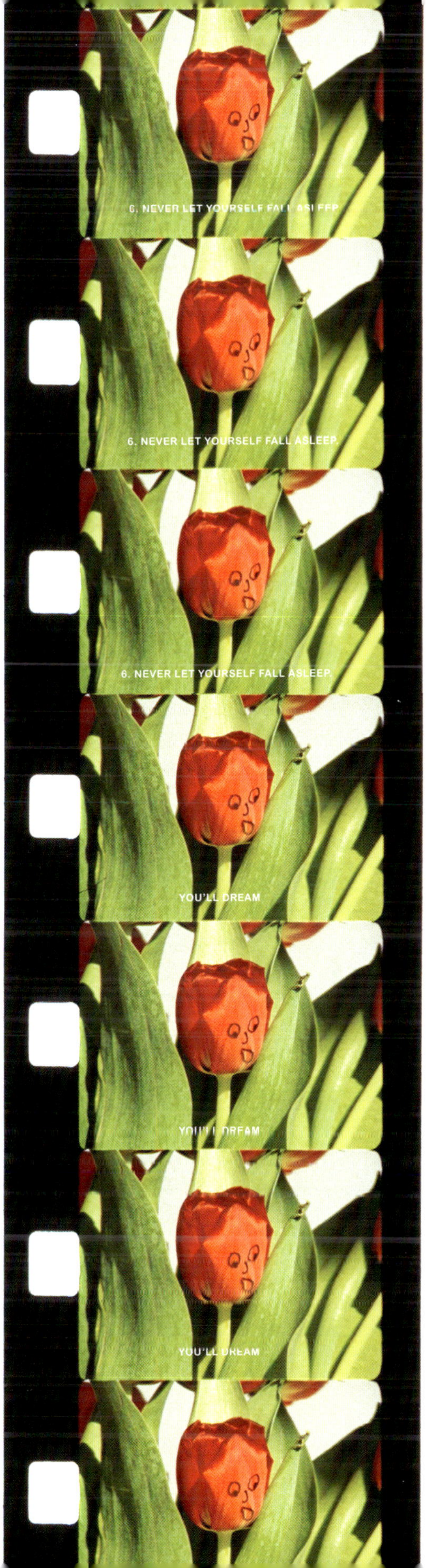

6. NEVER LET YOURSELF FALL ASLEEP.
6. NEVER LET YOURSELF FALL ASLEEP.
6. NEVER LET YOURSELF FALL ASLEEP.
YOU'LL DREAM
YOU'LL DREAM
YOU'LL DREAM

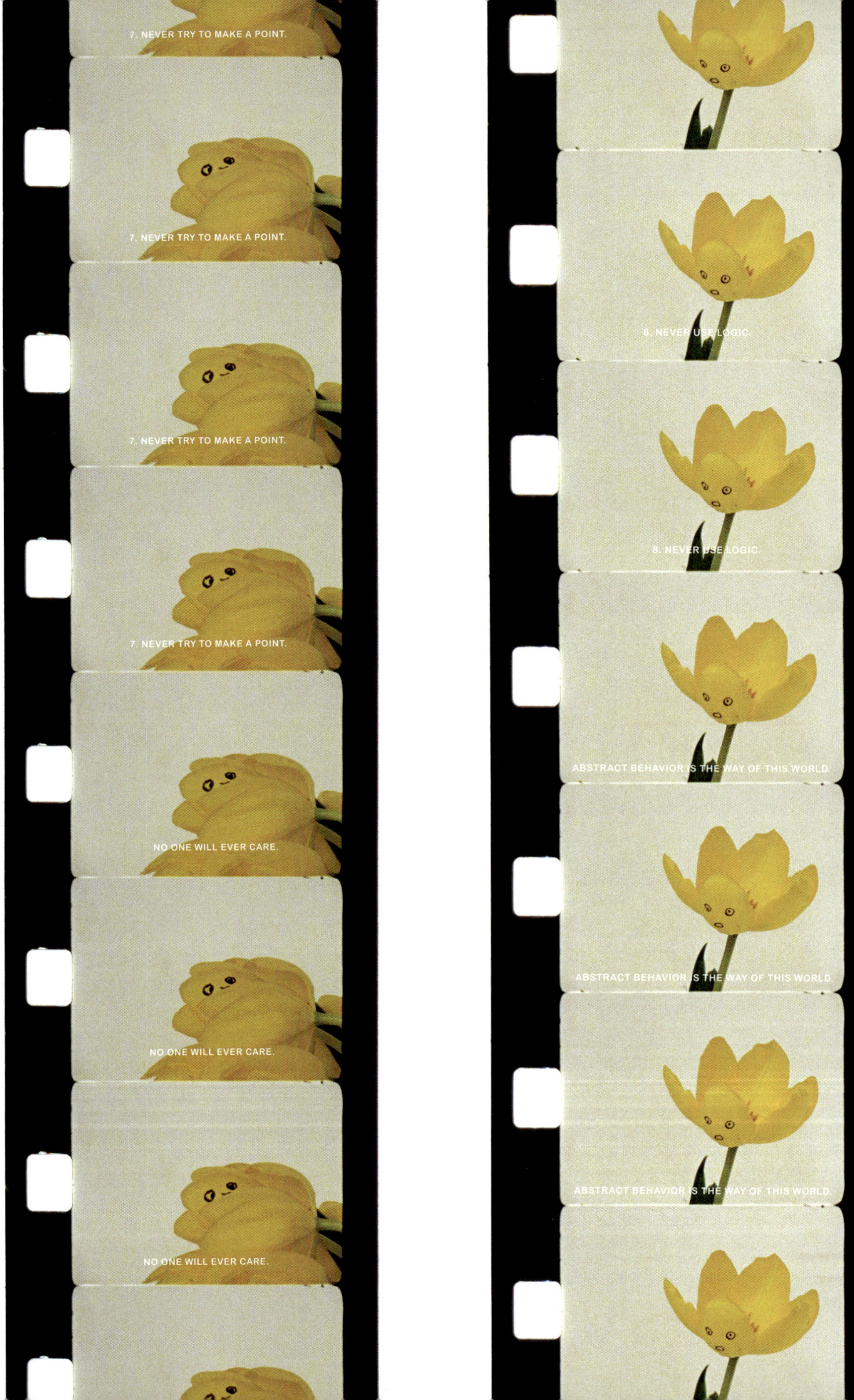

34

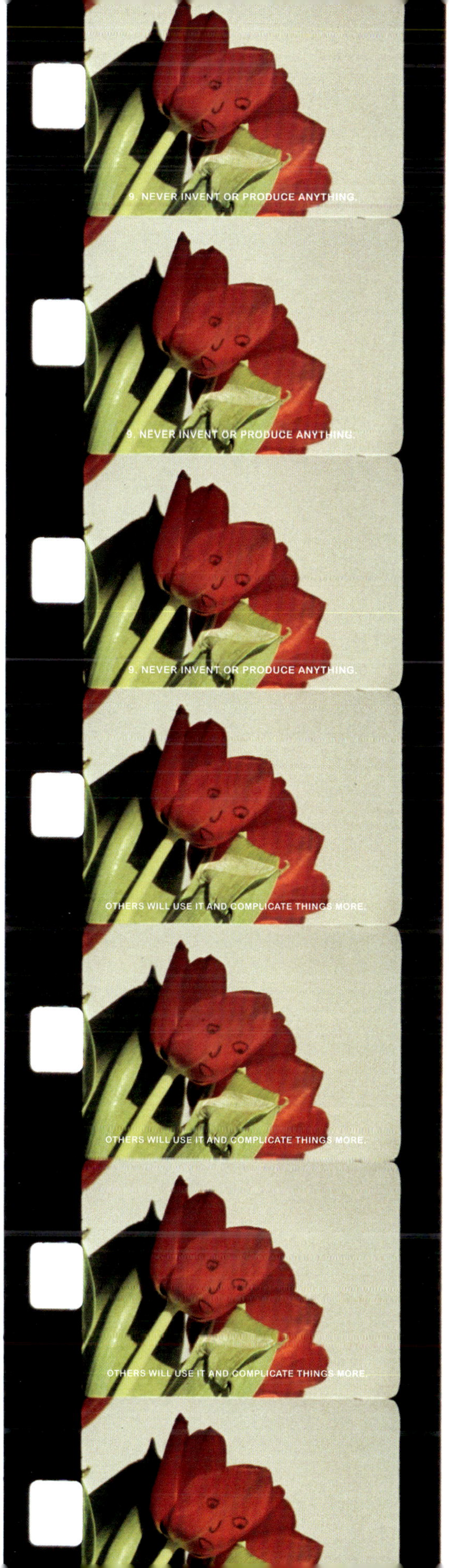

9. NEVER INVENT OR PRODUCE ANYTHING.
9. NEVER INVENT OR PRODUCE ANYTHING.
9. NEVER INVENT OR PRODUCE ANYTHING.
OTHERS WILL USE IT AND COMPLICATE THINGS MORE.
OTHERS WILL USE IT AND COMPLICATE THINGS MORE.
OTHERS WILL USE IT AND COMPLICATE THINGS MORE.
12. THINK OF DEATH AND THE DEAD EVERYDAY. 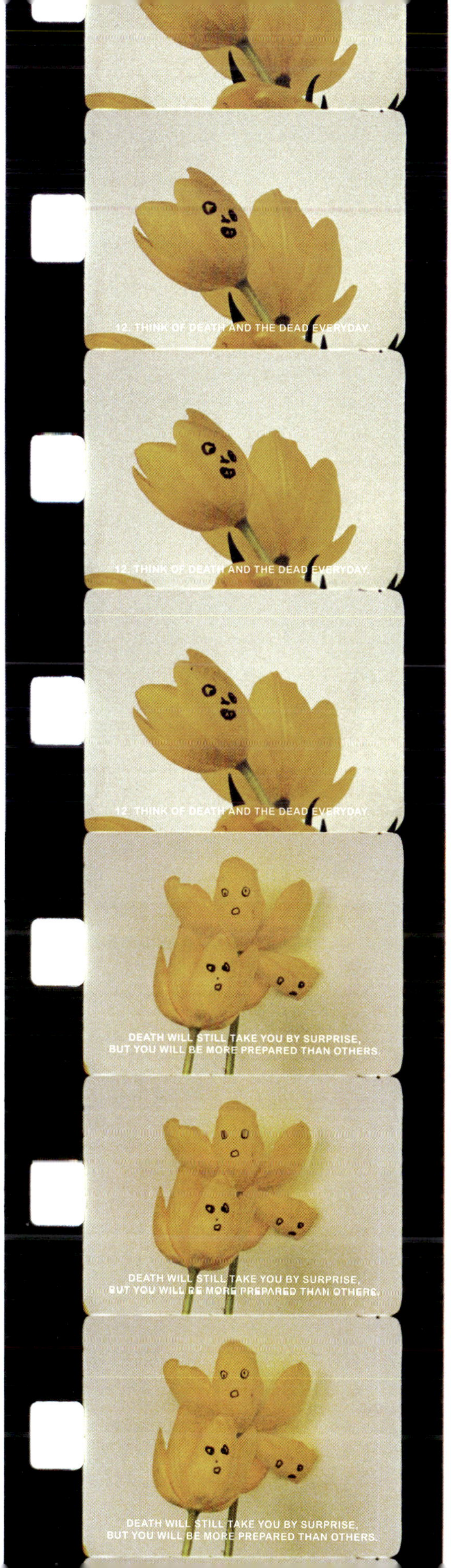
12. THINK OF DEATH AND THE DEAD EVERYDAY.
12. THINK OF DEATH AND THE DEAD EVERYDAY.
DEATH WILL STILL TAKE YOU BY SURPRISE,
BUT YOU WILL BE MORE PREPARED THAN OTHERS.
DEATH WILL STILL TAKE YOU BY SURPRISE,
BUT YOU WILL BE MORE PREPARED THAN OTHERS.
DEATH WILL STILL TAKE YOU BY SURPRISE,
BUT YOU WILL BE MORE PREPARED THAN OTHERS.

ETERNITY

2018

ACRYLIC, VINYL, AND TEXT.
DIMENSIONS VARIABLE.

INSTALLATION VIEW,
UNIVERSITY GALLERIES OF
ILLINOIS STATE UNIVERSITY.

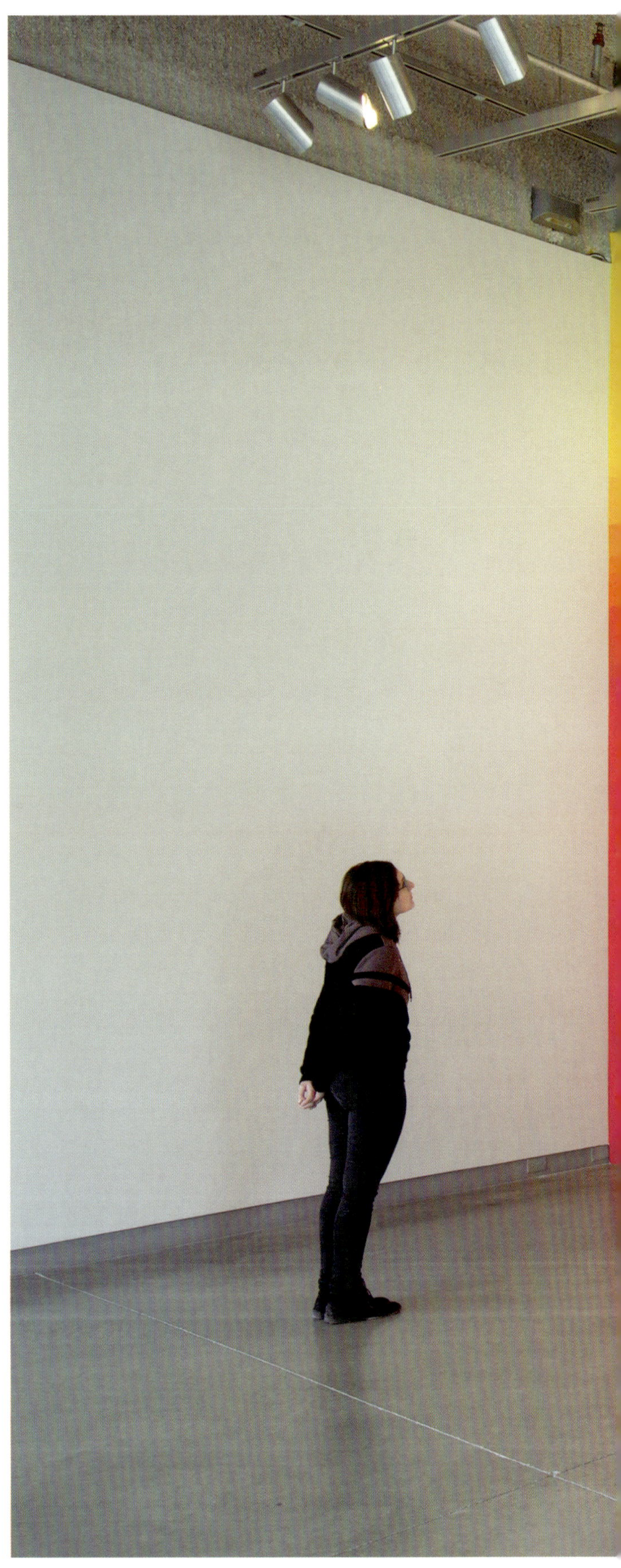

5500 YEARS OF DEATH, NICKNAMED "FATE"
WE TAKE SO MUCH FOR GRANTED. REMEMBER CARTHAGE? REMEMBER THE ELEPHANTS?
"I'M IN UNION SQUARE ABOUT TO GET ON THE TRAIN" LOUD TOURISTS AND AMBITIOUS DELUSIONISTS HIJACKED HER RUSHED VOICE
TIME SHRINKS INTO A SHAPESHIFTING SOAP BUBBLE
FLOATING. GOODBYE ETERNITY
MAY WE ALL BREED CONTINUOUSLY FOREVER

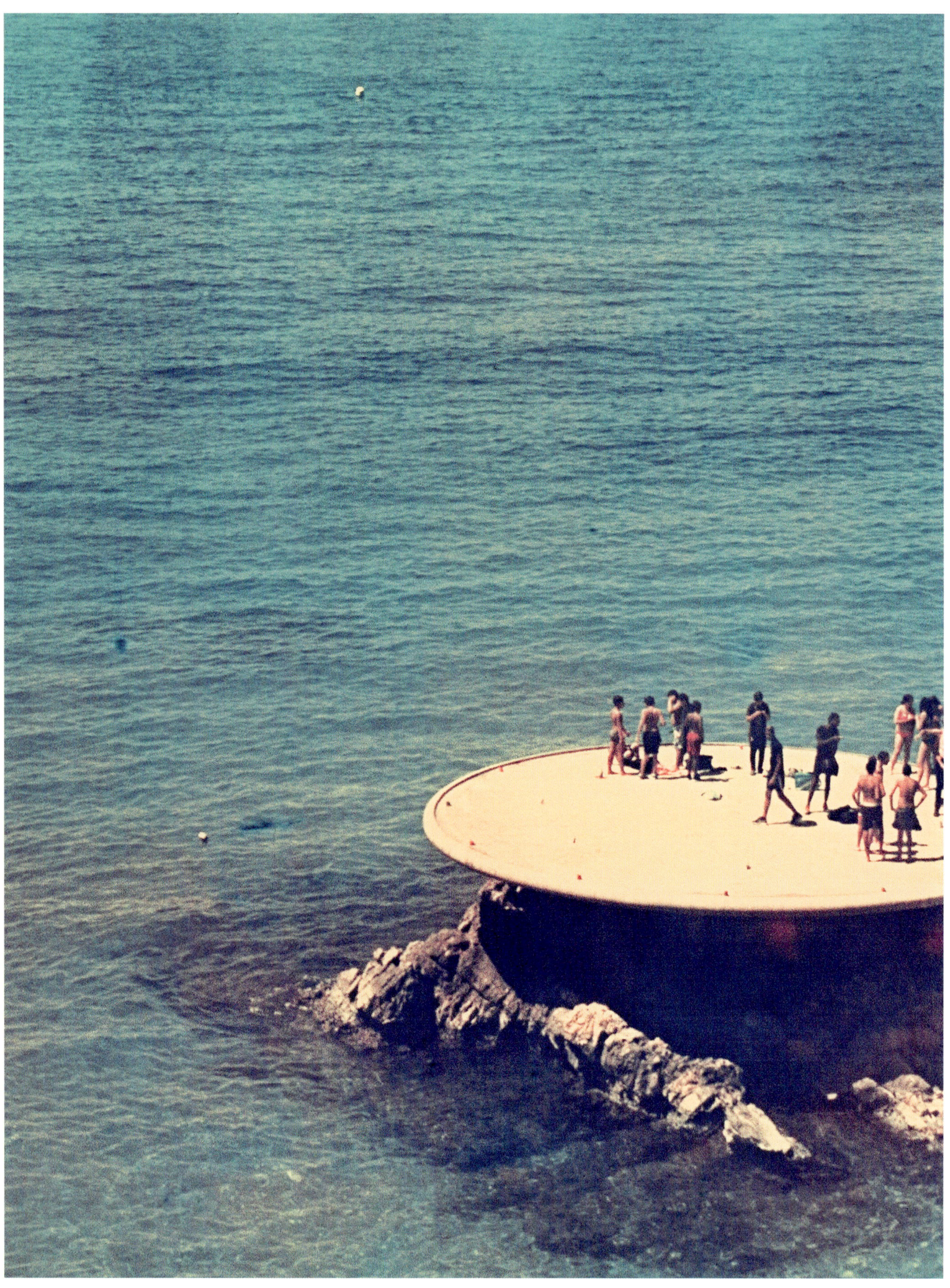

FOR SEVENTY YEARS THE GHOSTS OF THE FISHERMEN, THEIR WIVES AND THEIR PET CATS DWELLED IN TUCKED AWAY WARM COAT SLEEVES. IT WAS TIME TO RETURN HOME.

An excerpt from the script of *The Dent*, 2014.

THE DENT

2014

SUPER 16MM FILM
TRANSFERRED TO FULL
HD VIDEO.

19:02 MINUTES

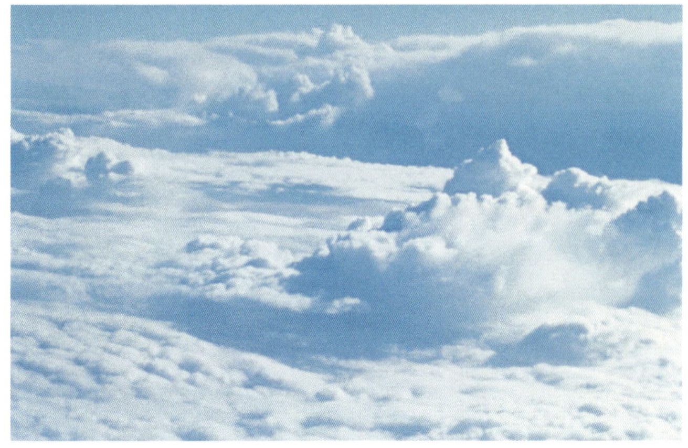

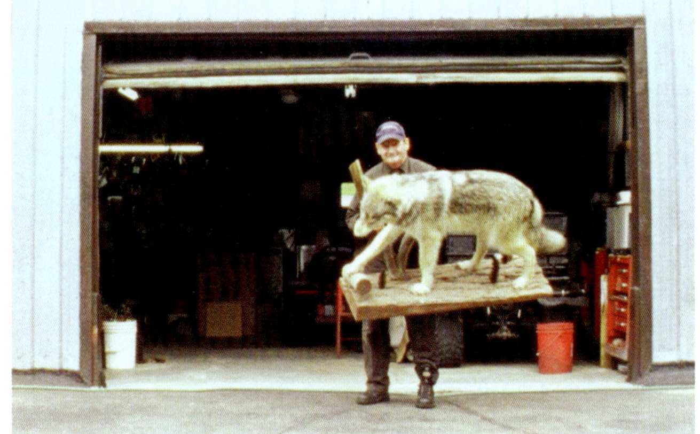

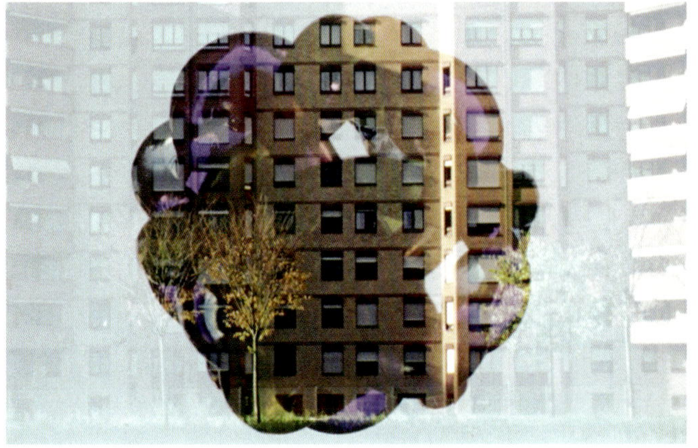

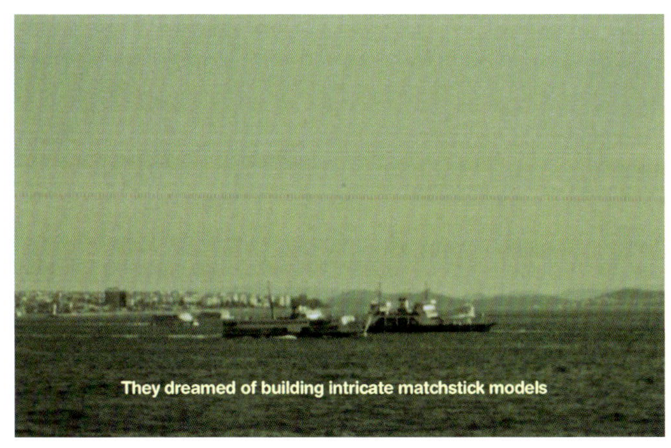
They dreamed of building intricate matchstick models

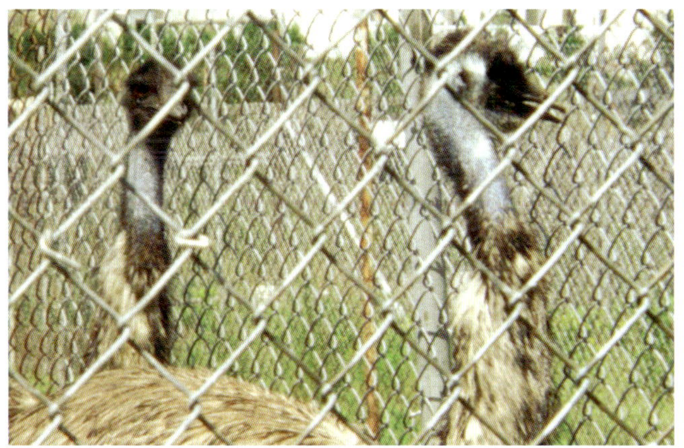

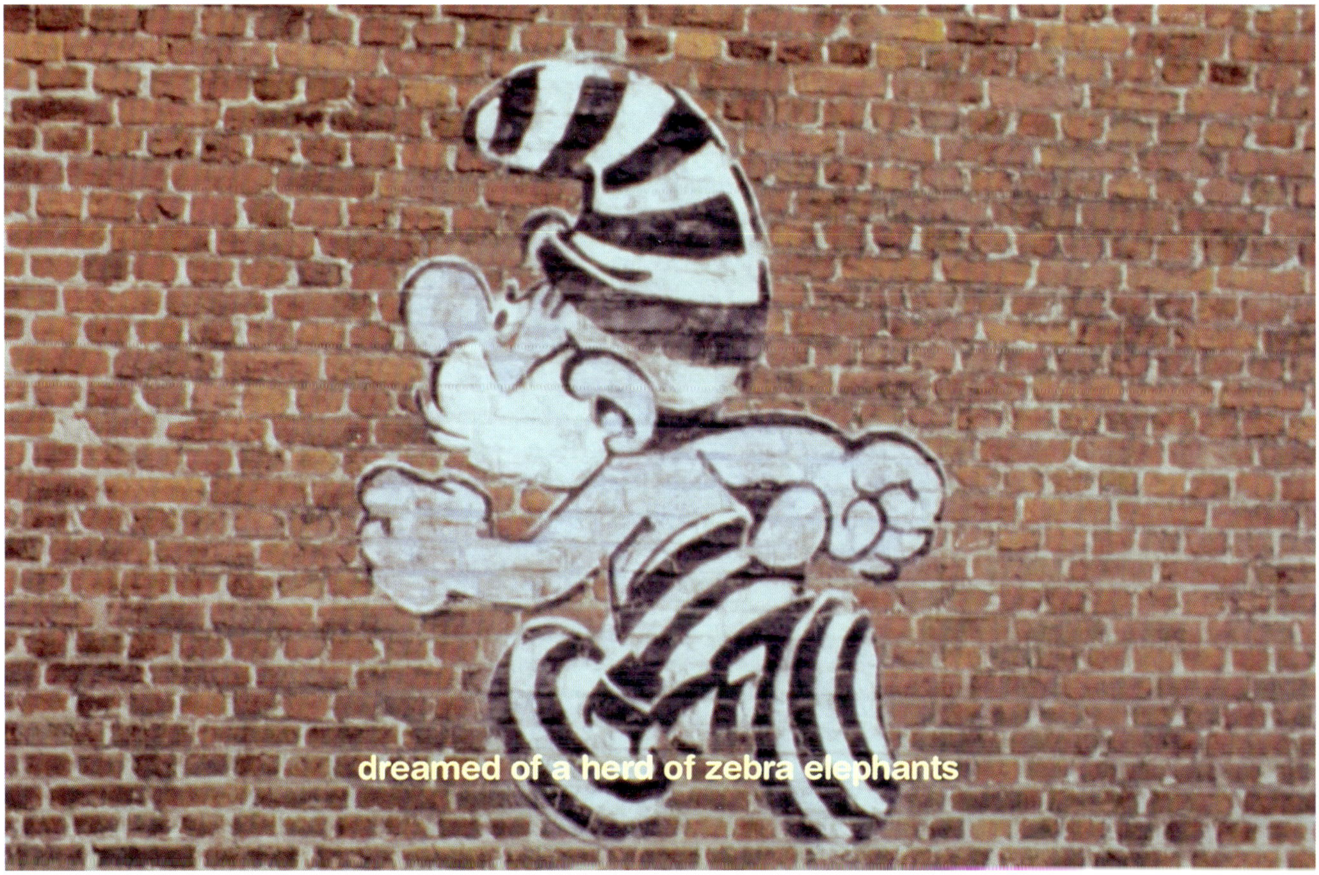

dreamed of a herd of zebra elephants

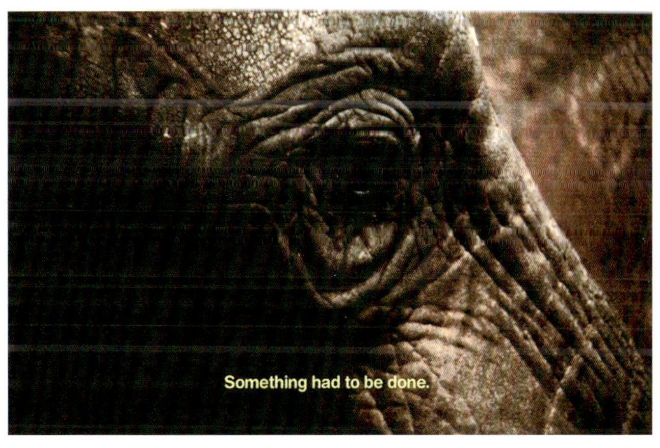
Something had to be done.

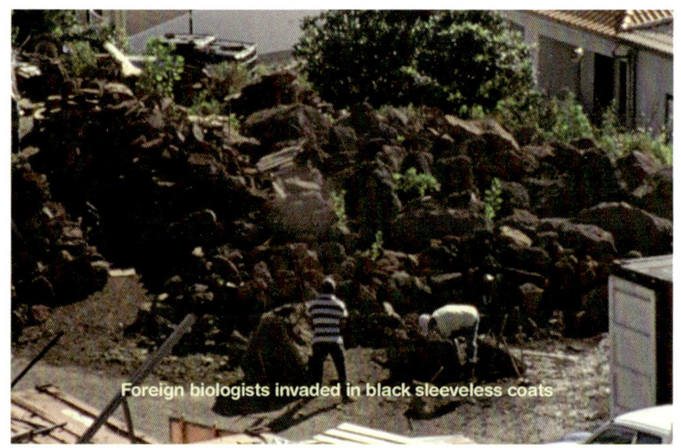
Foreign biologists invaded in black sleeveless coats

42

of force-feeding the truth.

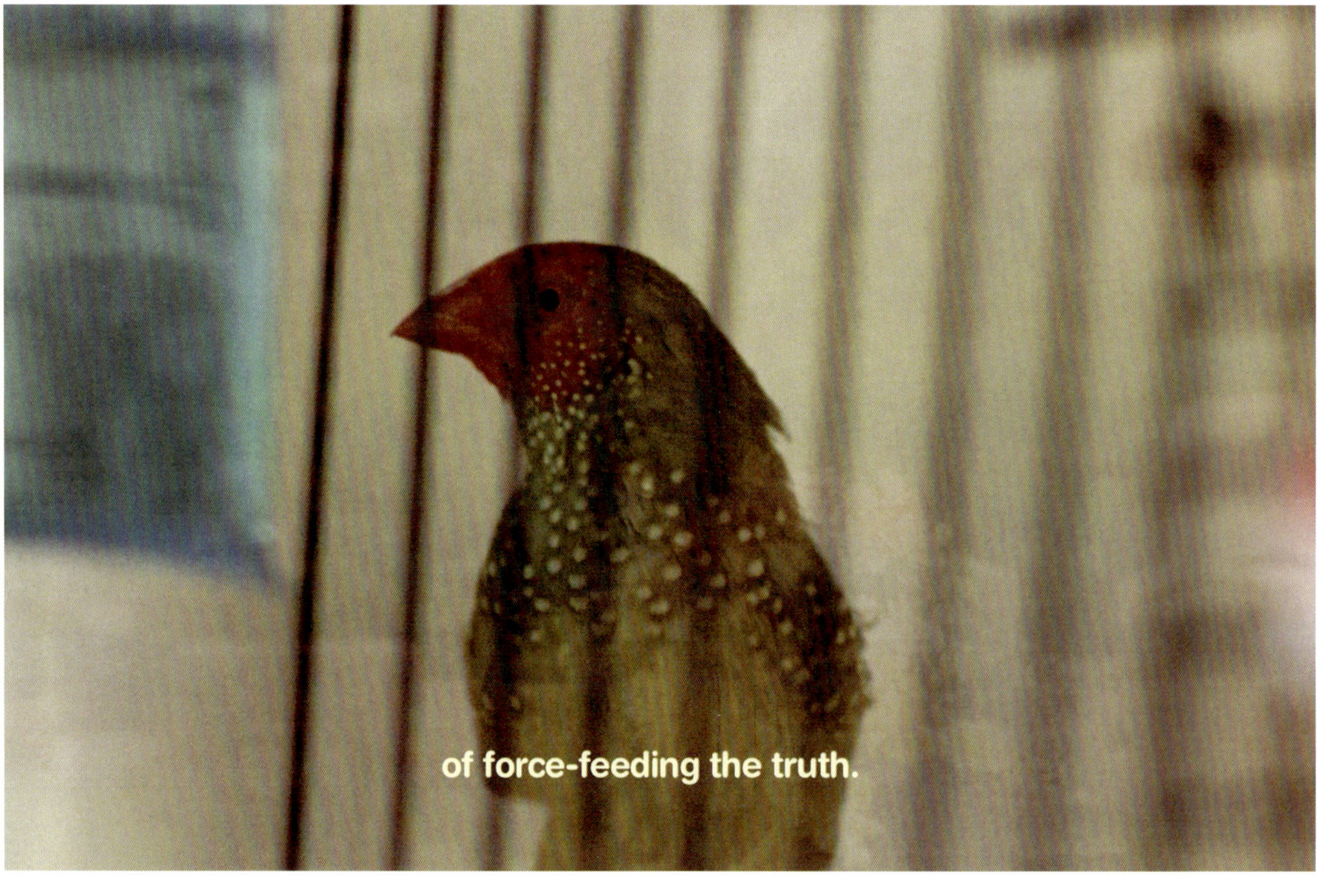

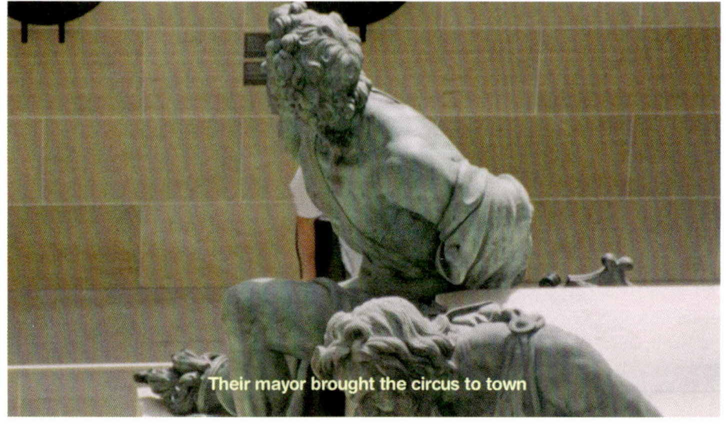
Their mayor brought the circus to town

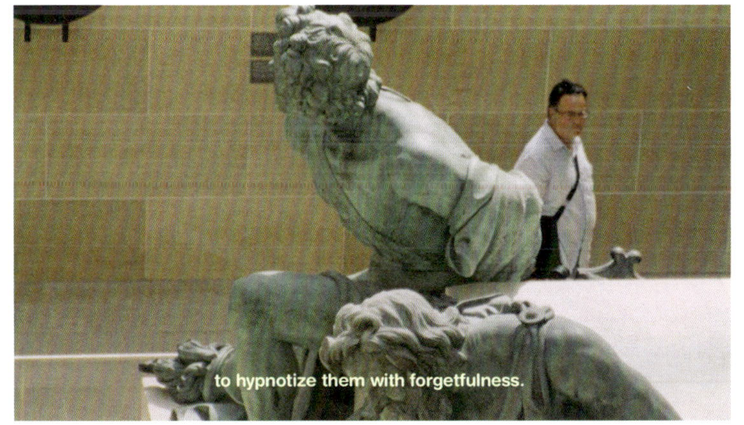

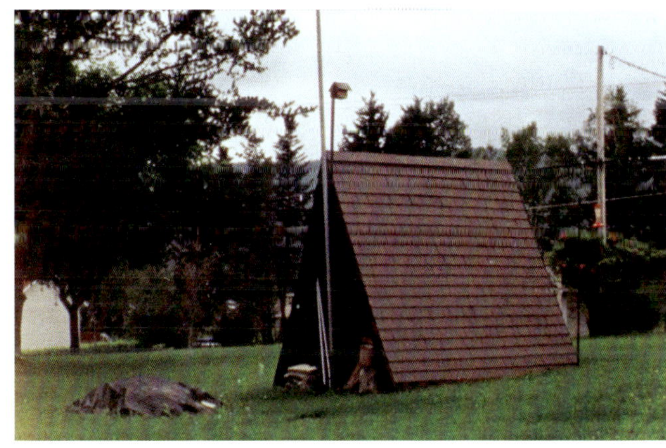

43

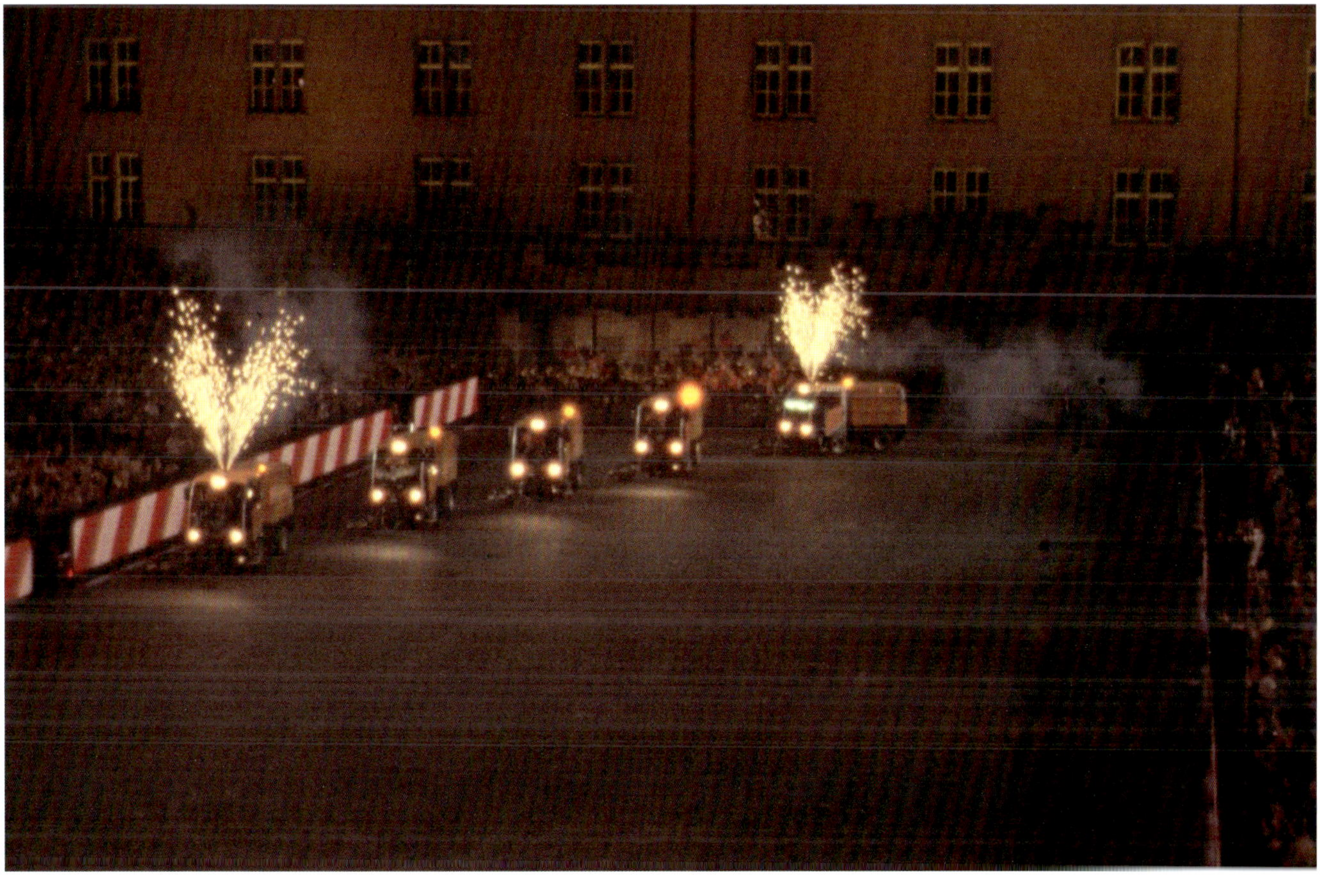

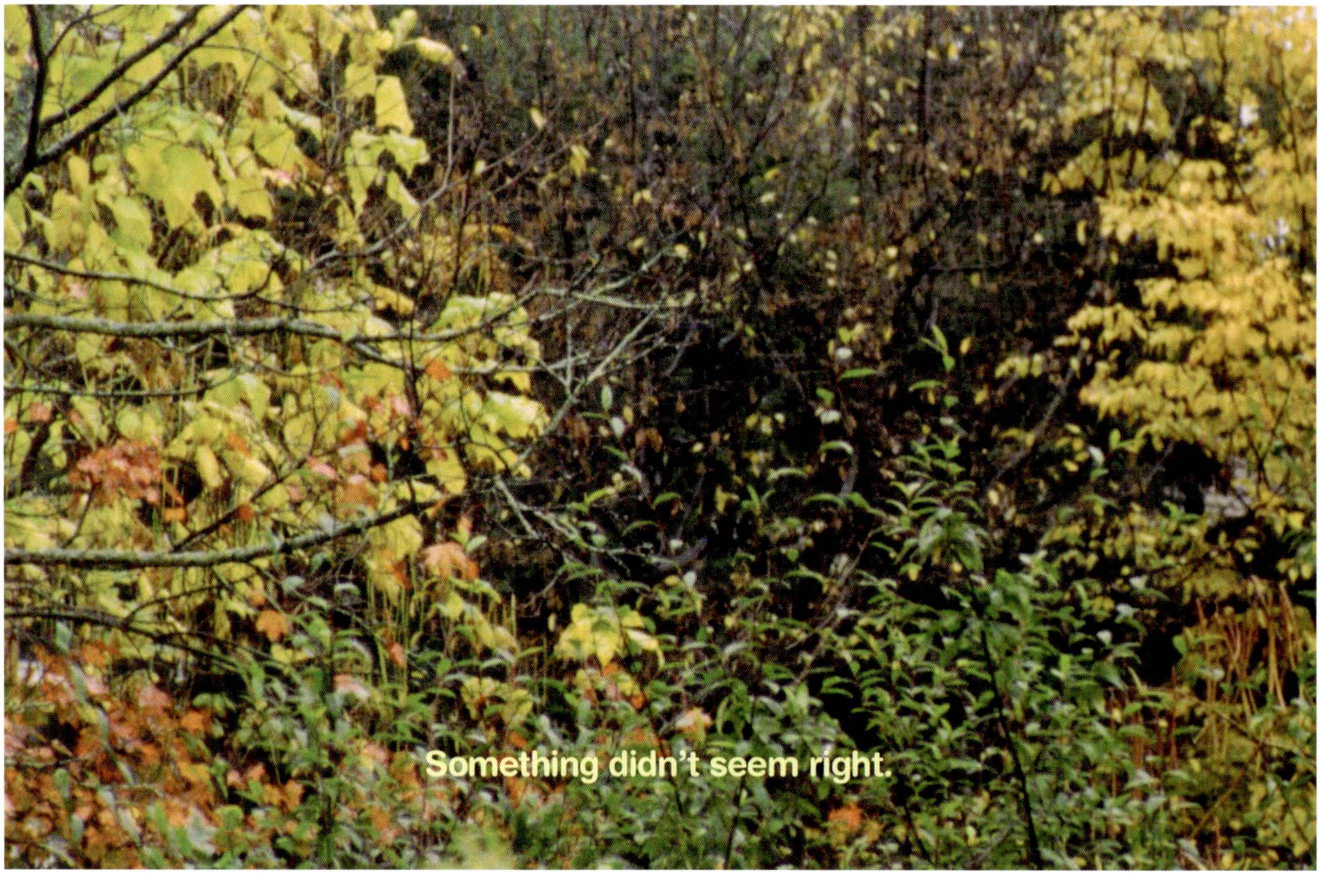

Something didn't seem right.

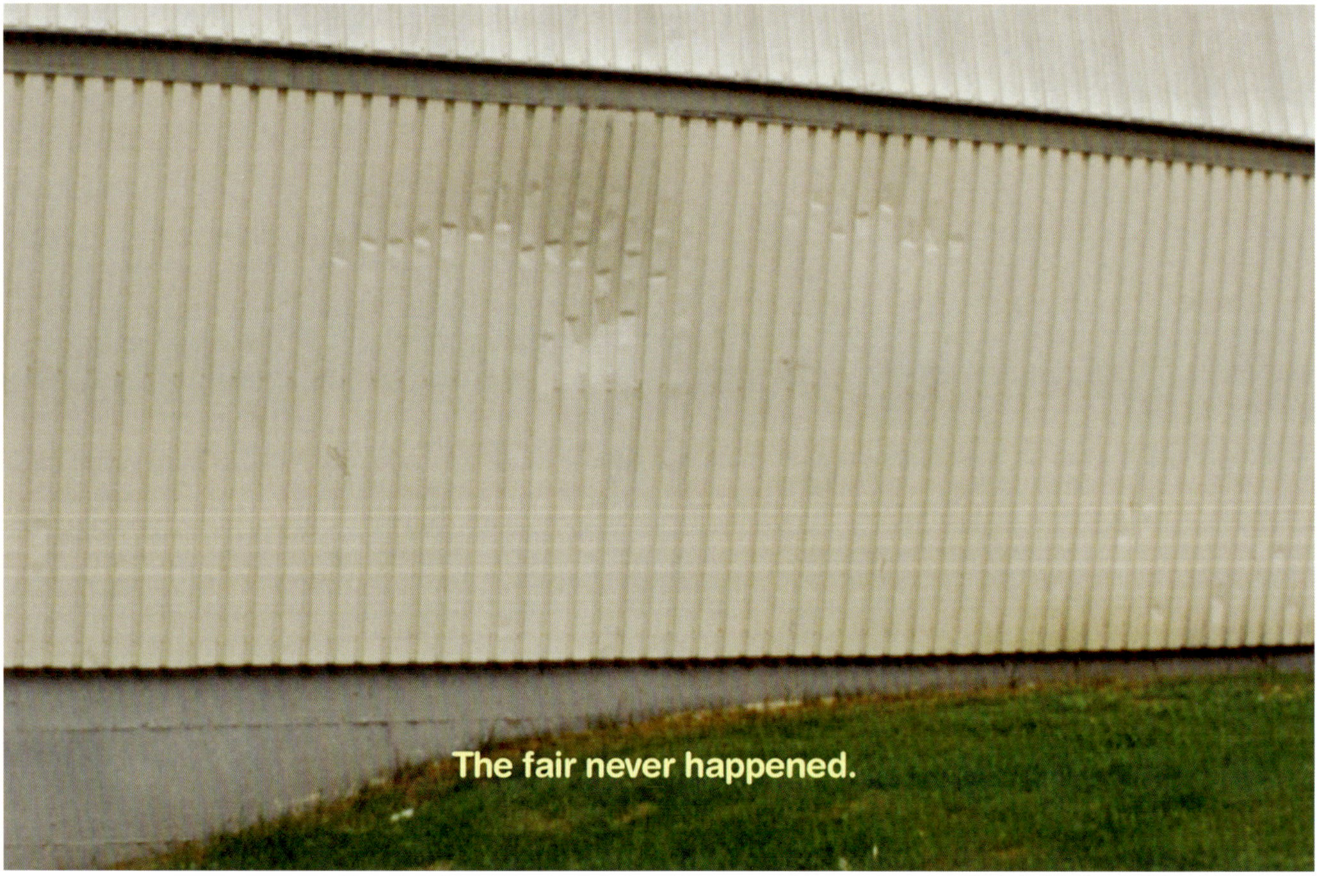

The fair never happened.

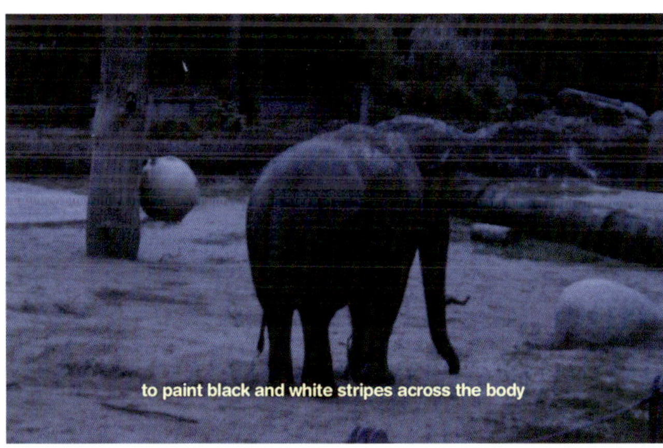

to paint black and white stripes across the body

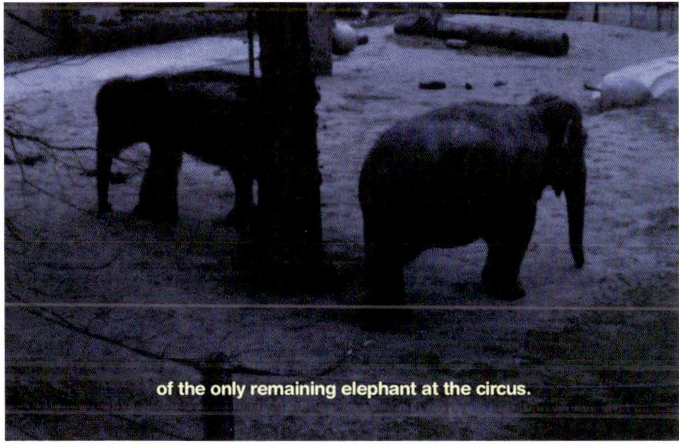

of the only remaining elephant at the circus.

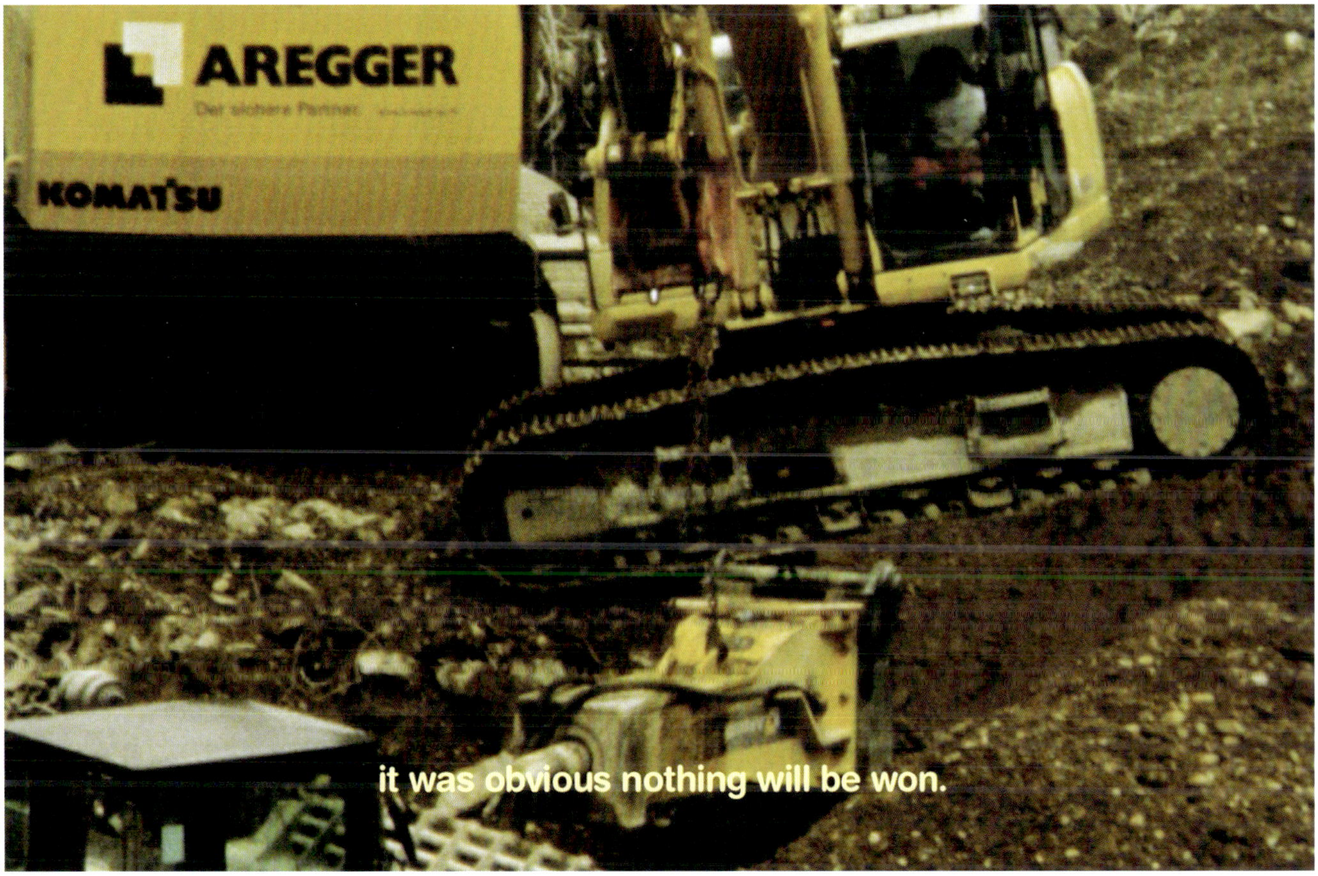

AREGGER
Der sichere Partner.
KOMATSU
it was obvious nothing will be won.

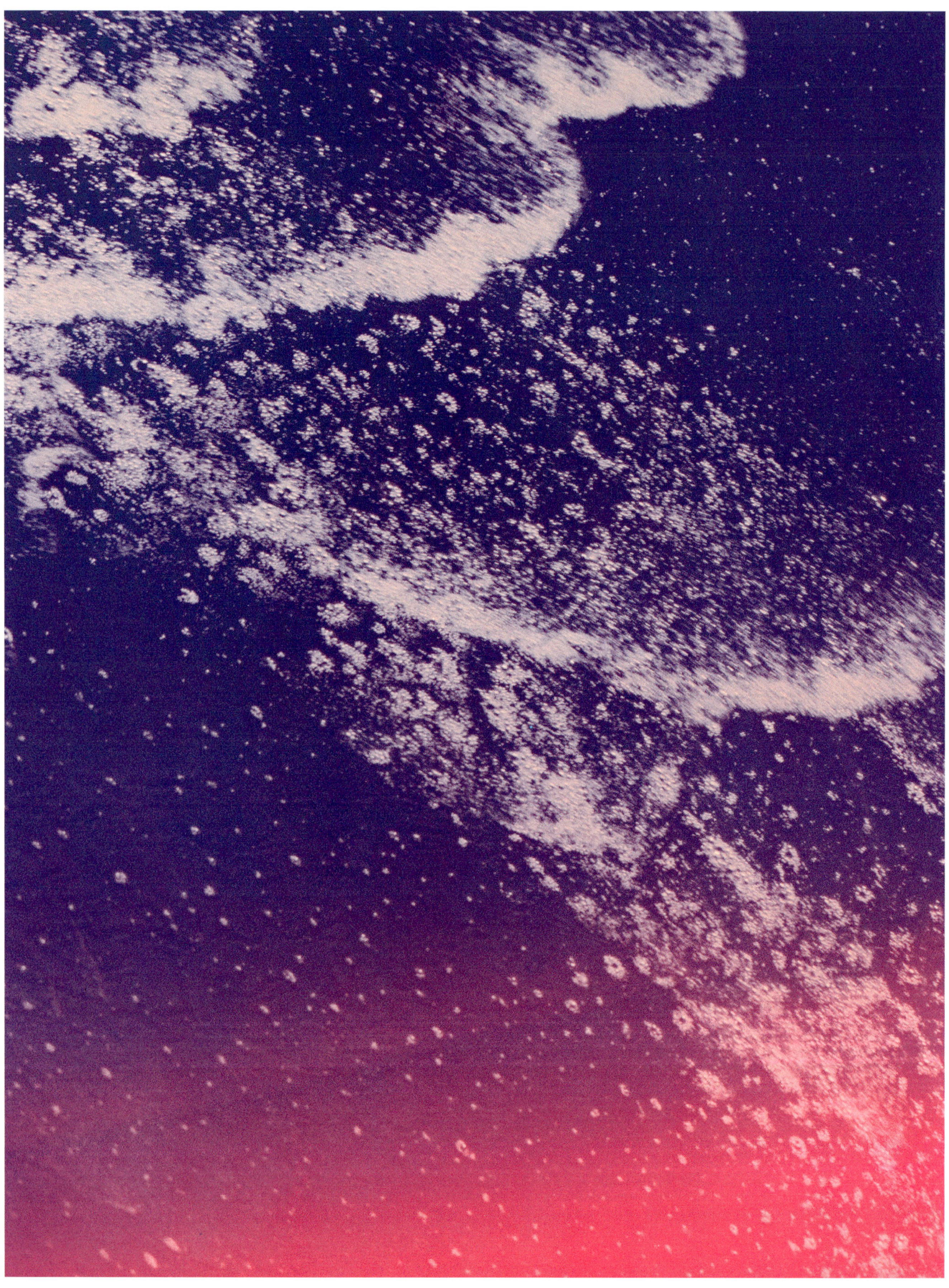

THOSE WATERFALLS?
YES I'VE SEEN THEM BEFORE.
IS THIS WHERE THE
WATER COMES FROM?
HE IS JUST THROWING UP.
WHAT?
THE DEVIL...
WHAT DO YOU MEAN?
THE WATERFALLS. THE DEVIL
IS THROWING THEM UP.
YOU MEAN FROM HIS
MOUTH?
YES.

An excerpt from the script of *The Many Colors of the Sky Radiate Forgetfulness*, 2014.

**THE MANY COLORS OF
THE SKY RADIATE
FORGETFULNESS**

2014

SUPER 16MM FILM
TRANSFERRED TO FULL
HD VIDEO.

11:09 MINUTES

48

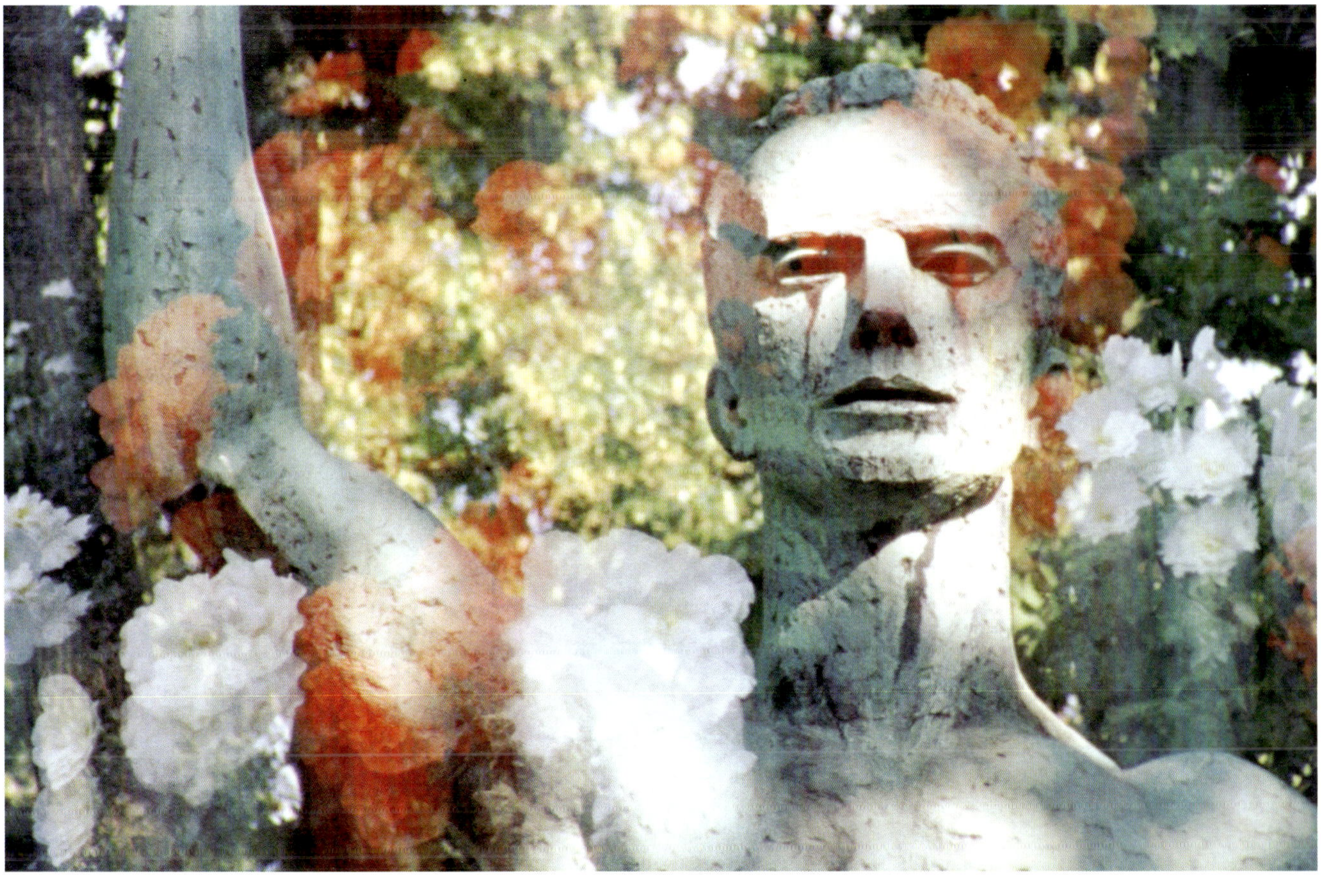

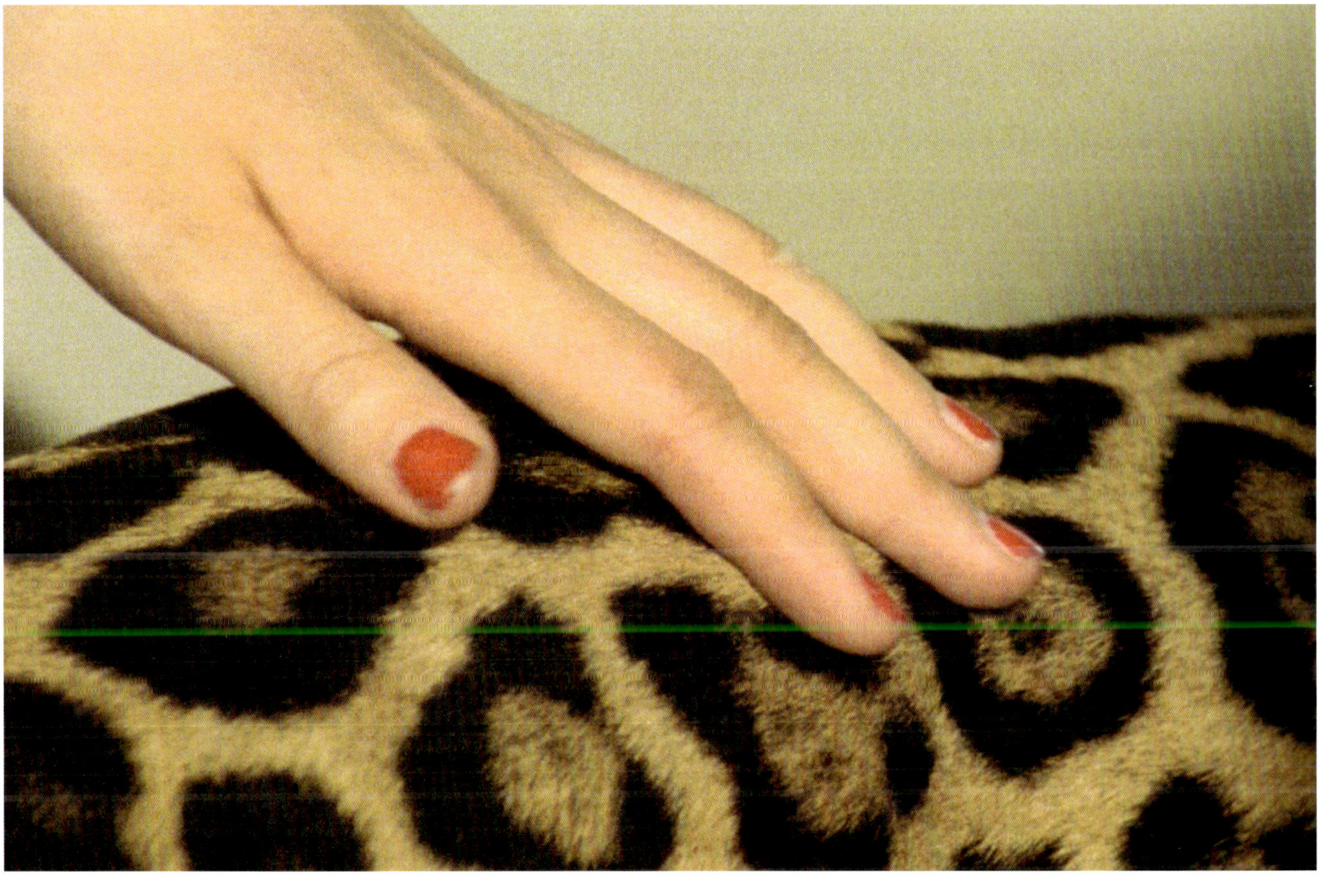

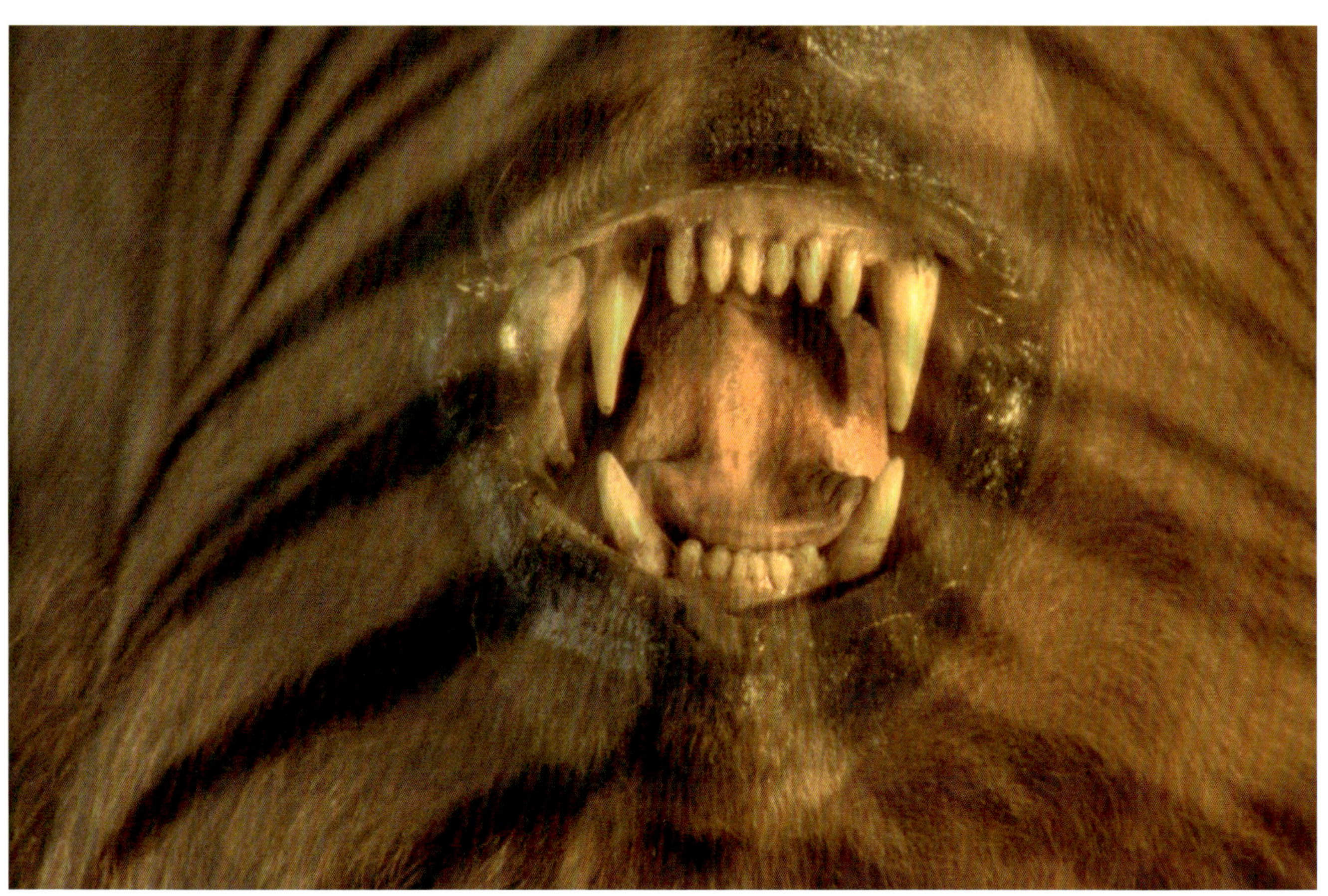

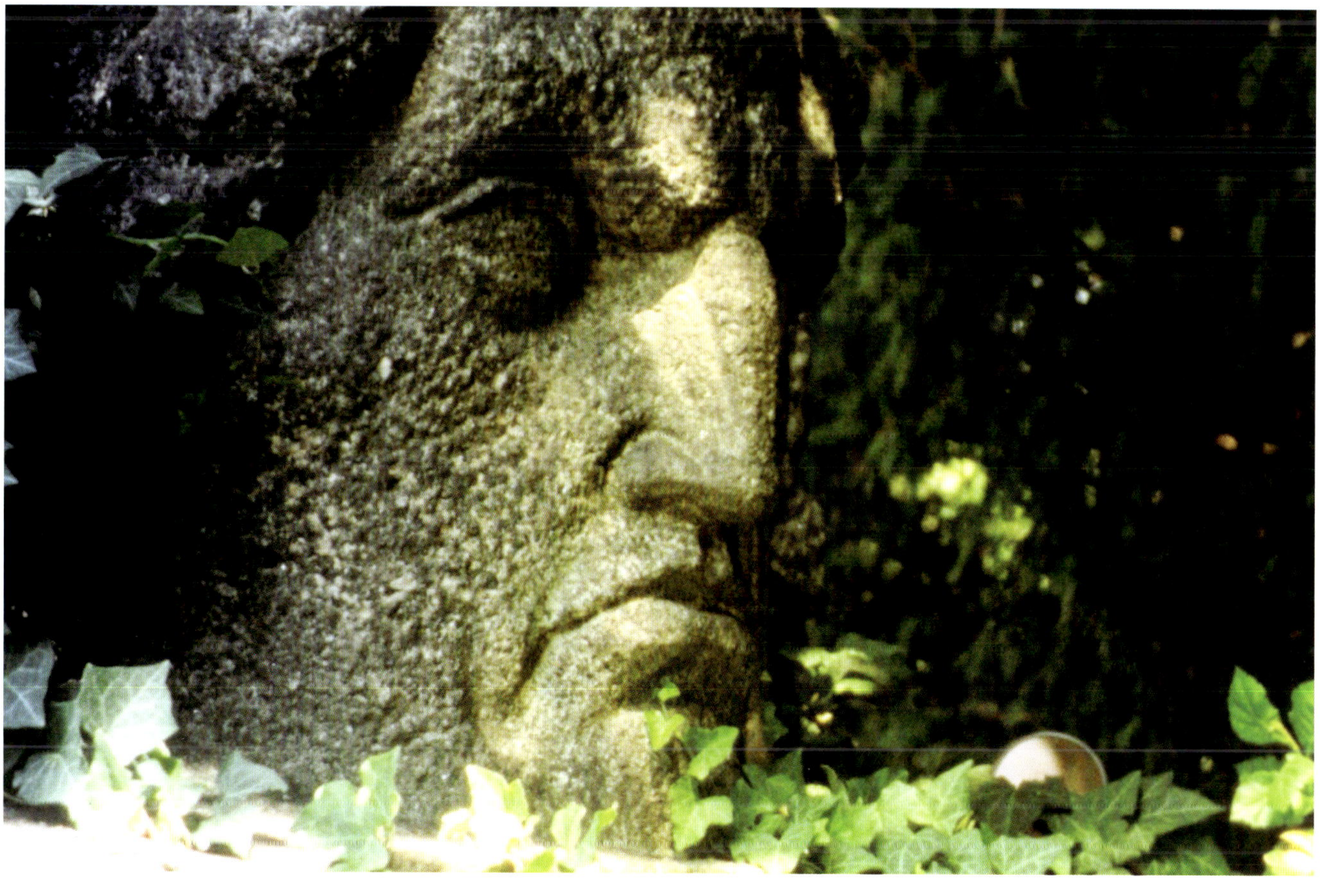

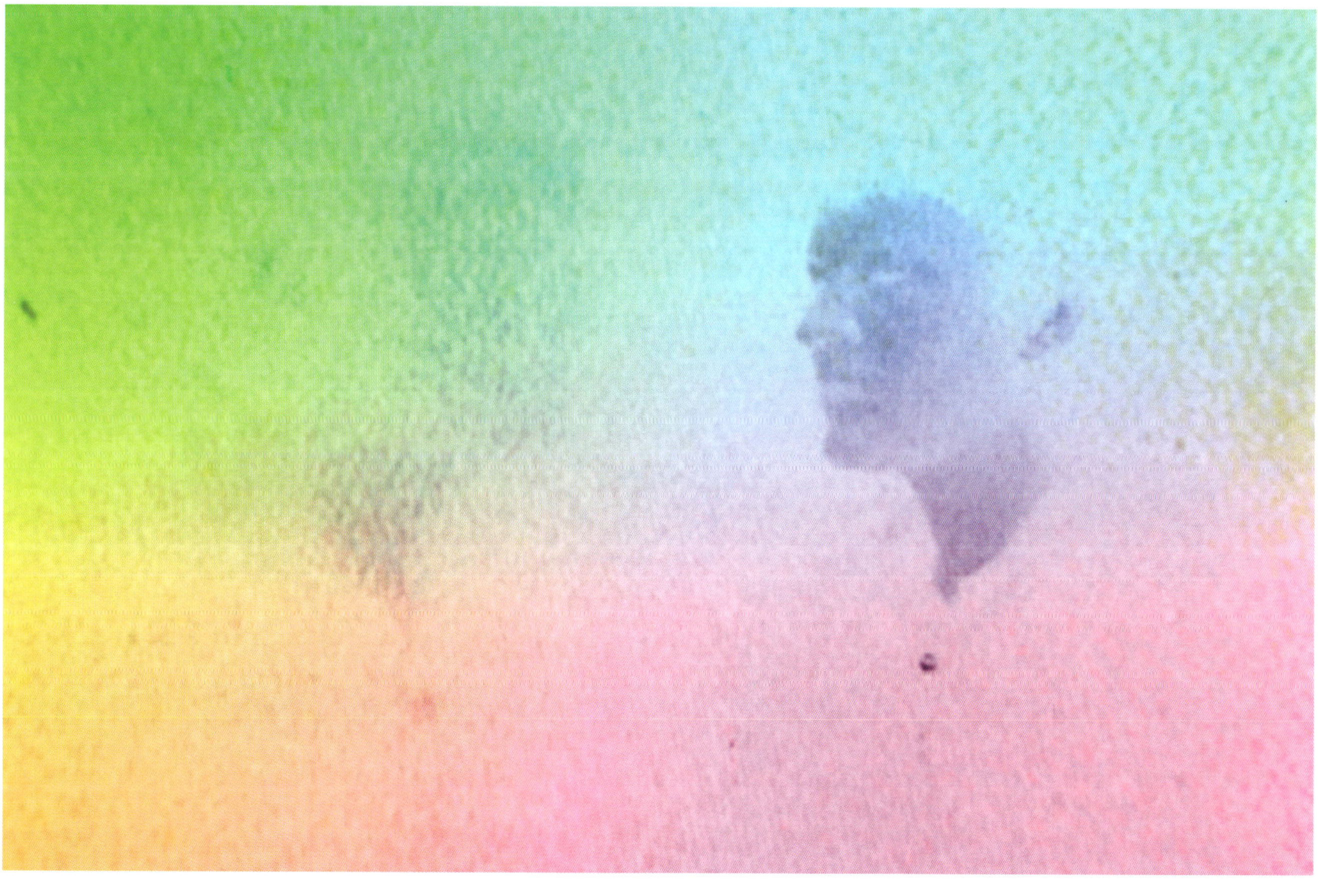

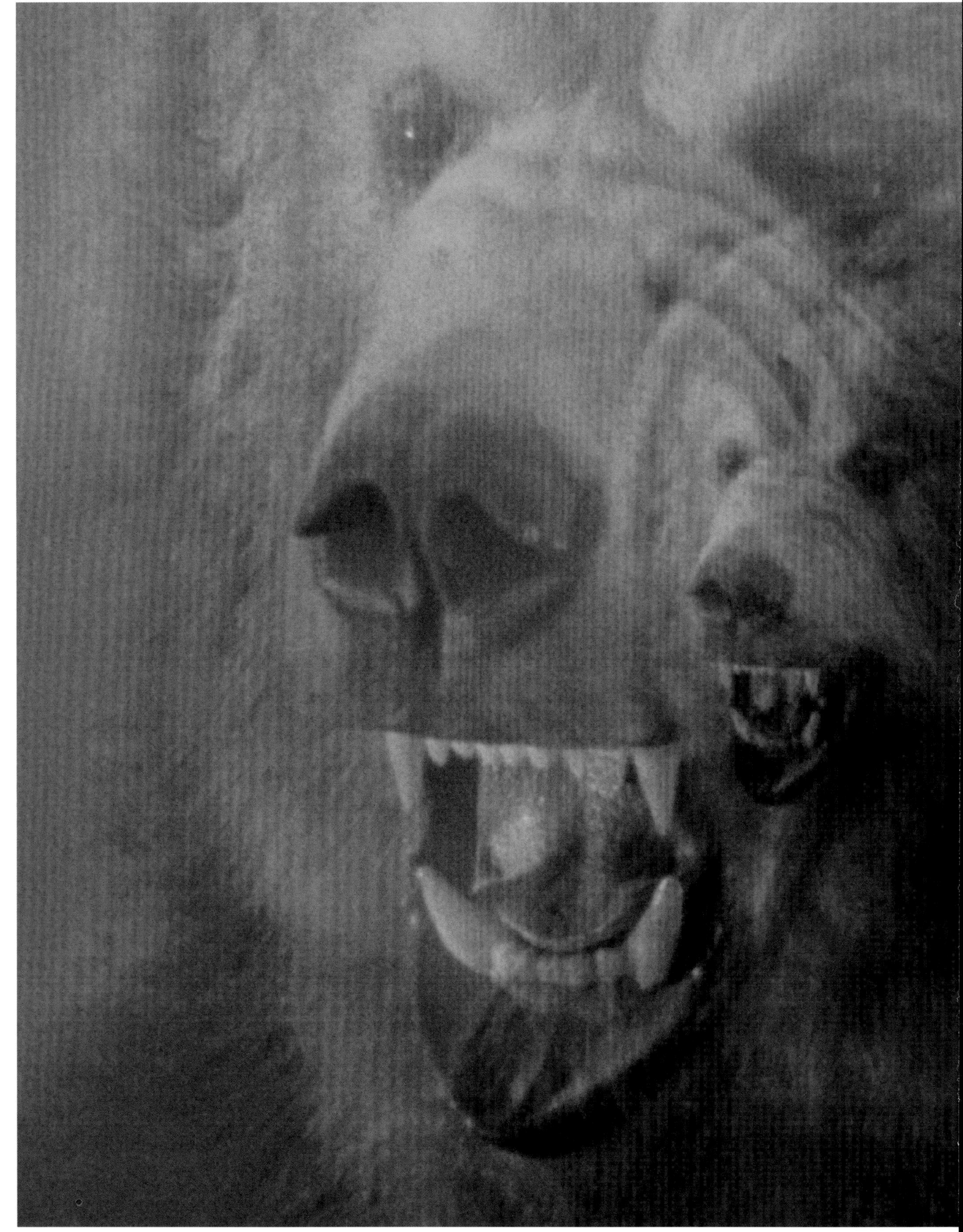

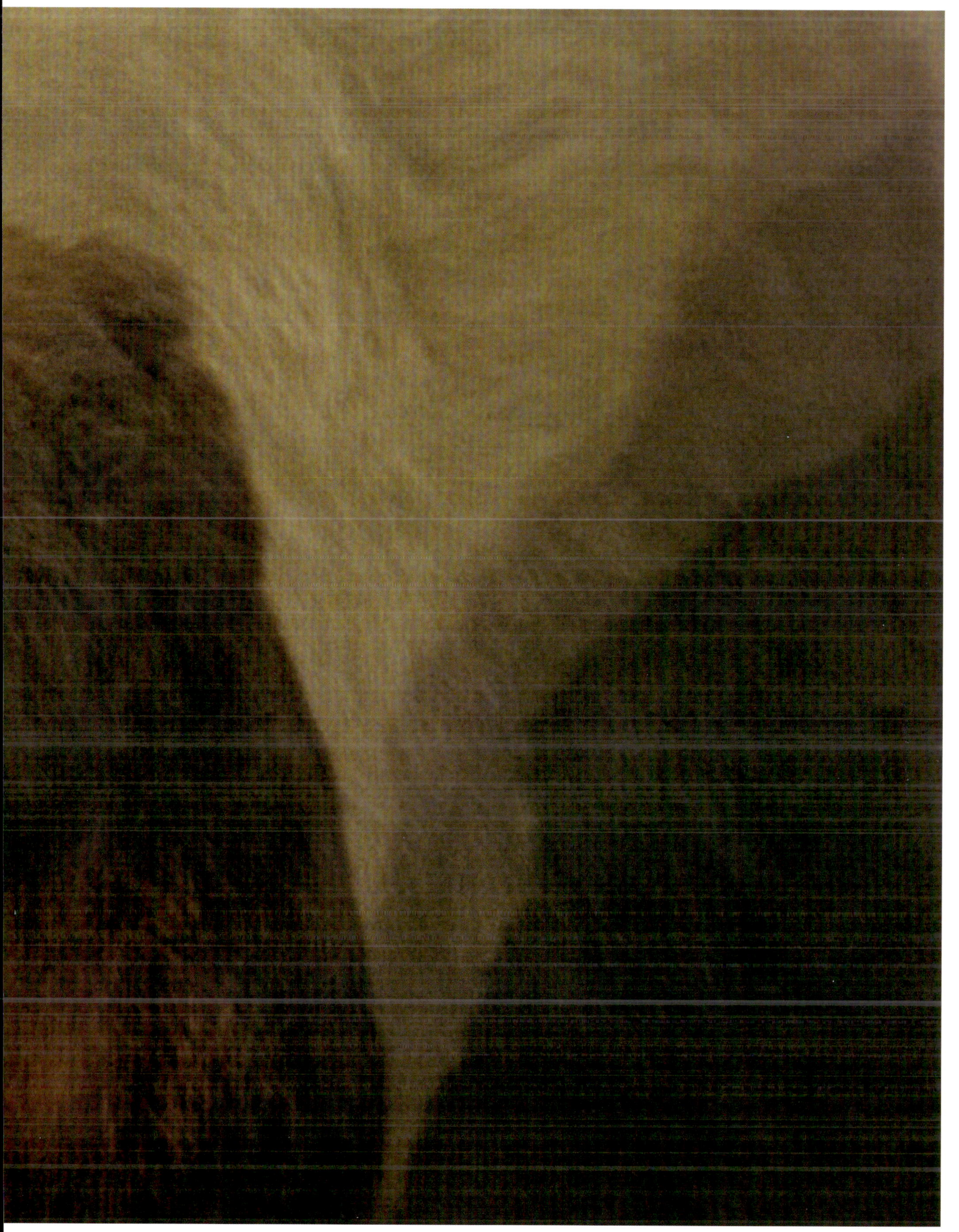

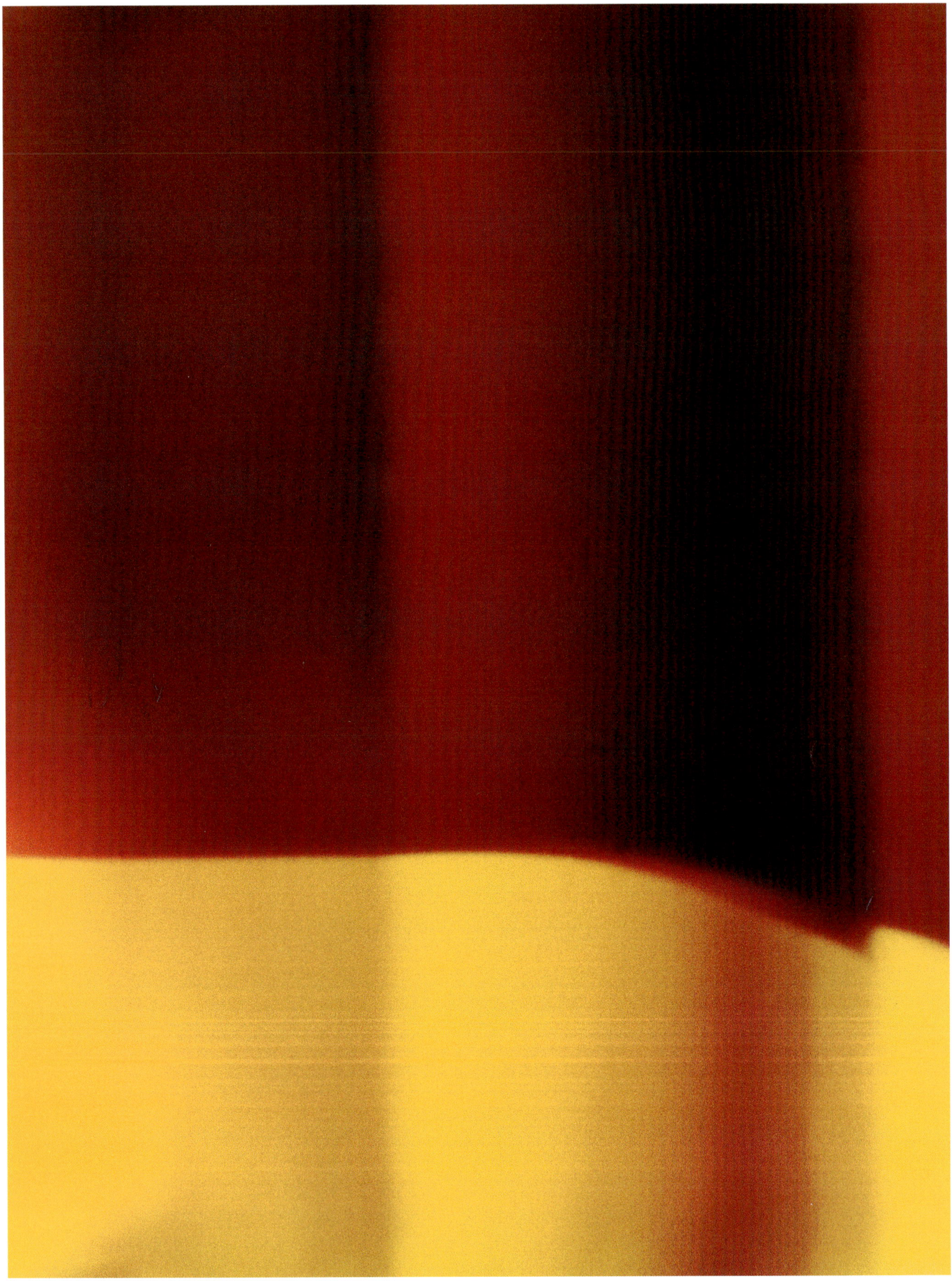

**WE'RE ALL VICTIMS OF
OUR OWN ADOPTED
FANTASIES HERE.
ALL THAT'S TAKEN US
CENTURIES TO ACCOMPLISH
IS PROVING USELESS.
ANY BRANCH OUTSIDE YOUR
WINDOW HAD A BETTER
LIFE THAN ANY OF US.
AND YOU'RE CALLING TO ASK
ABOUT REALITY?
A QUINCE PIE IS REALITY.
THE FRUIT NO ONE EATS IS
REALITY.**

An excerpt from the script of *The Everyday Ritual of Solitude Hatching Monkeys*, 2014.

THE EVERYDAY RITUAL OF SOLITUDE HATCHING MONKEYS

2014

SUPER 16MM FILM TRANSFERRED TO FULL HD VIDEO.

13:22 MINUTES

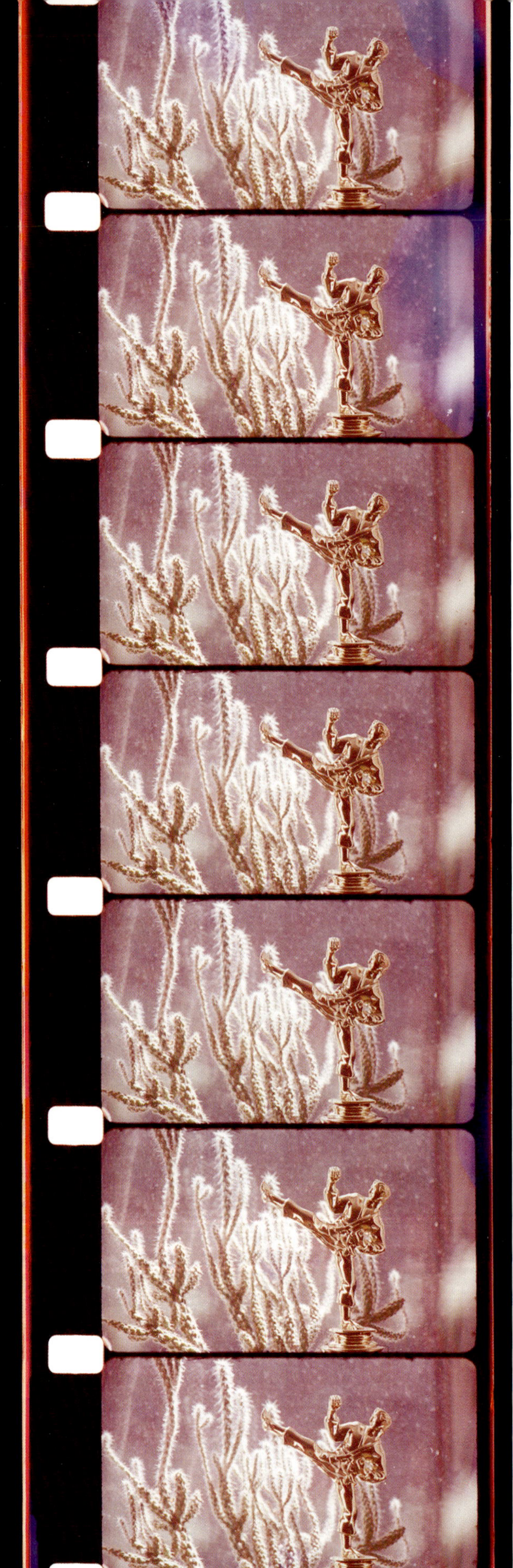

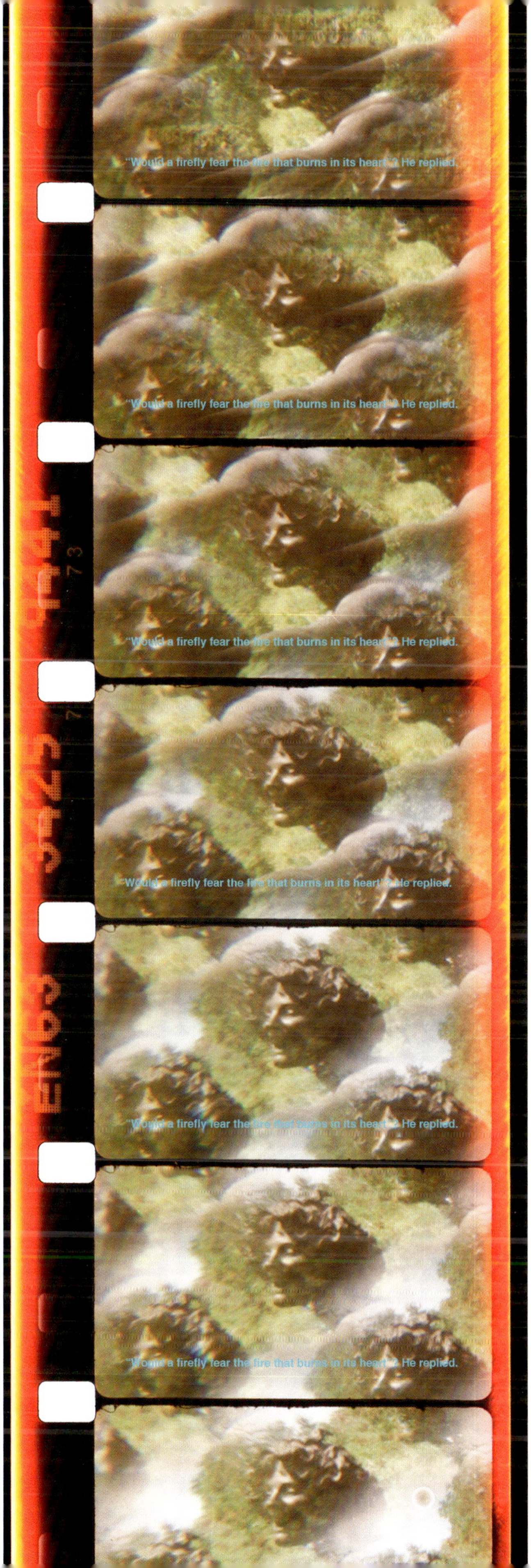

"Would a firefly fear the fire that burns in its heart?" He replied.

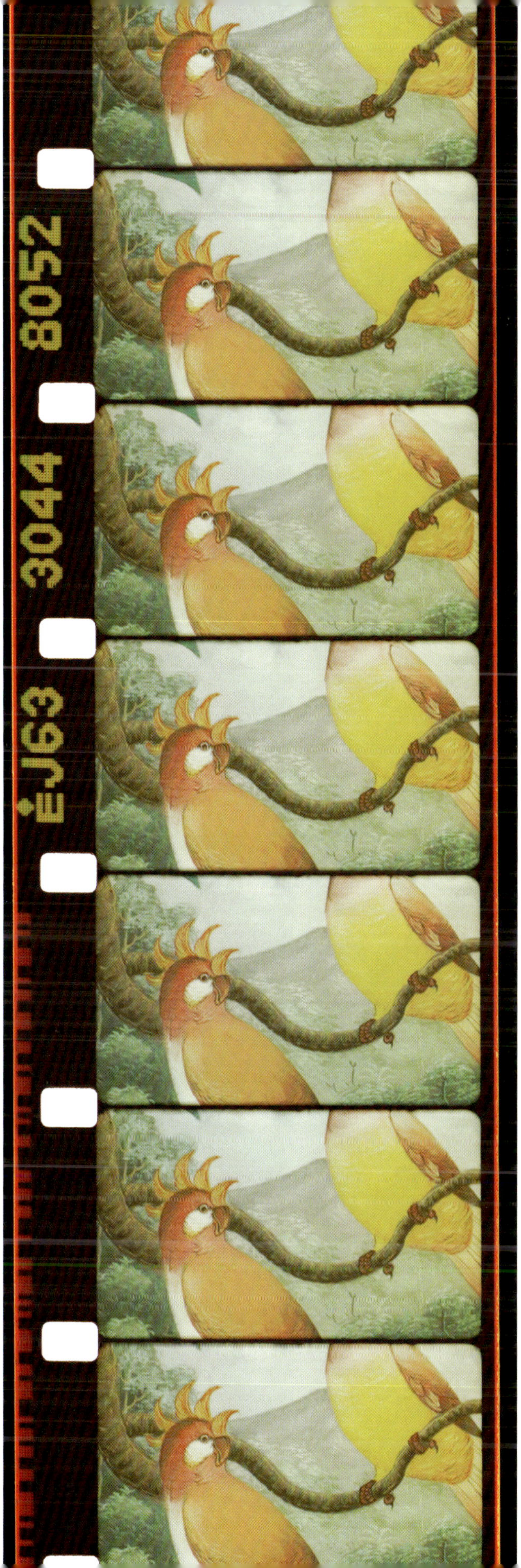

He stared at the coffee patterns in search of a prophecy

58

The ones who refuse to forget.

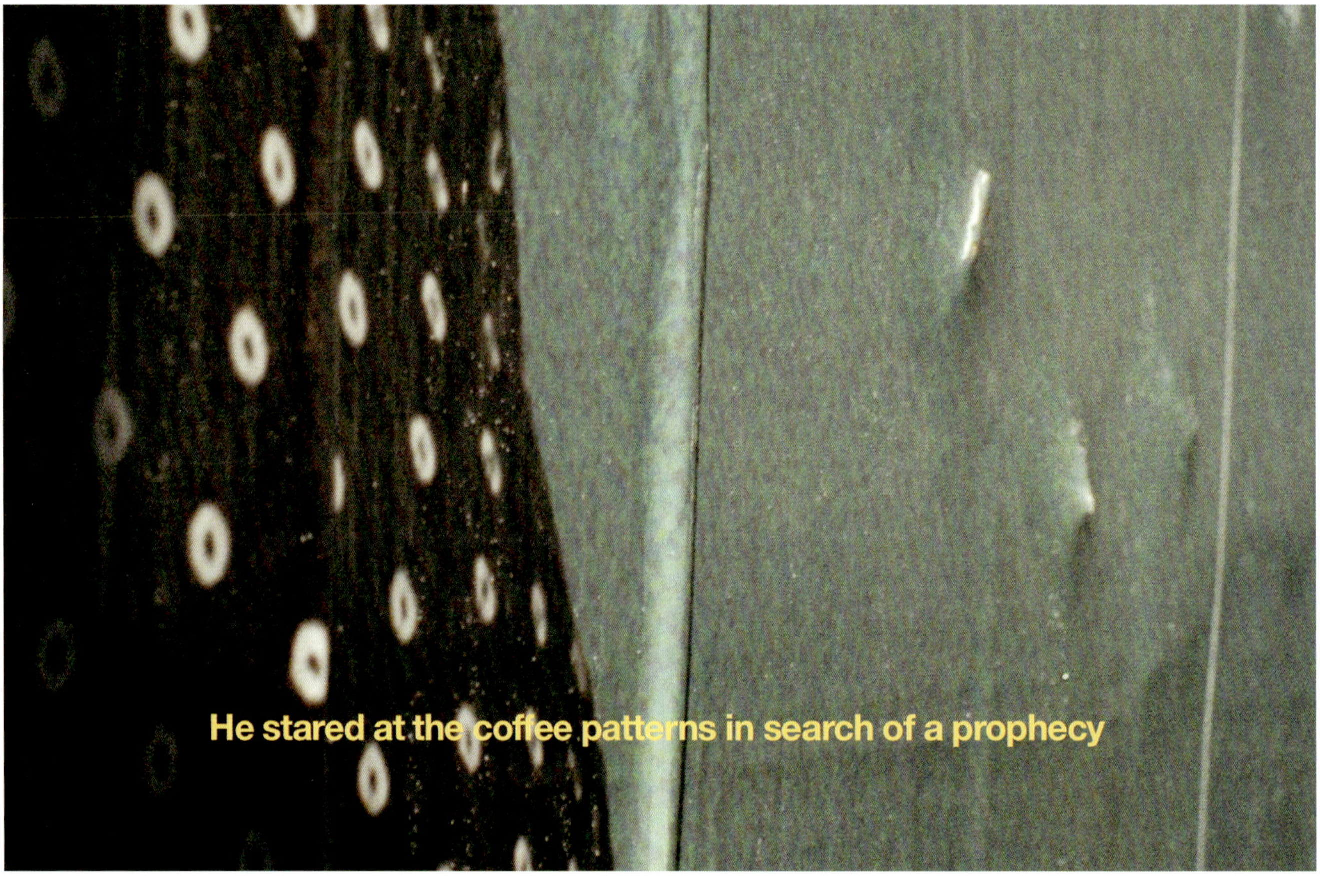

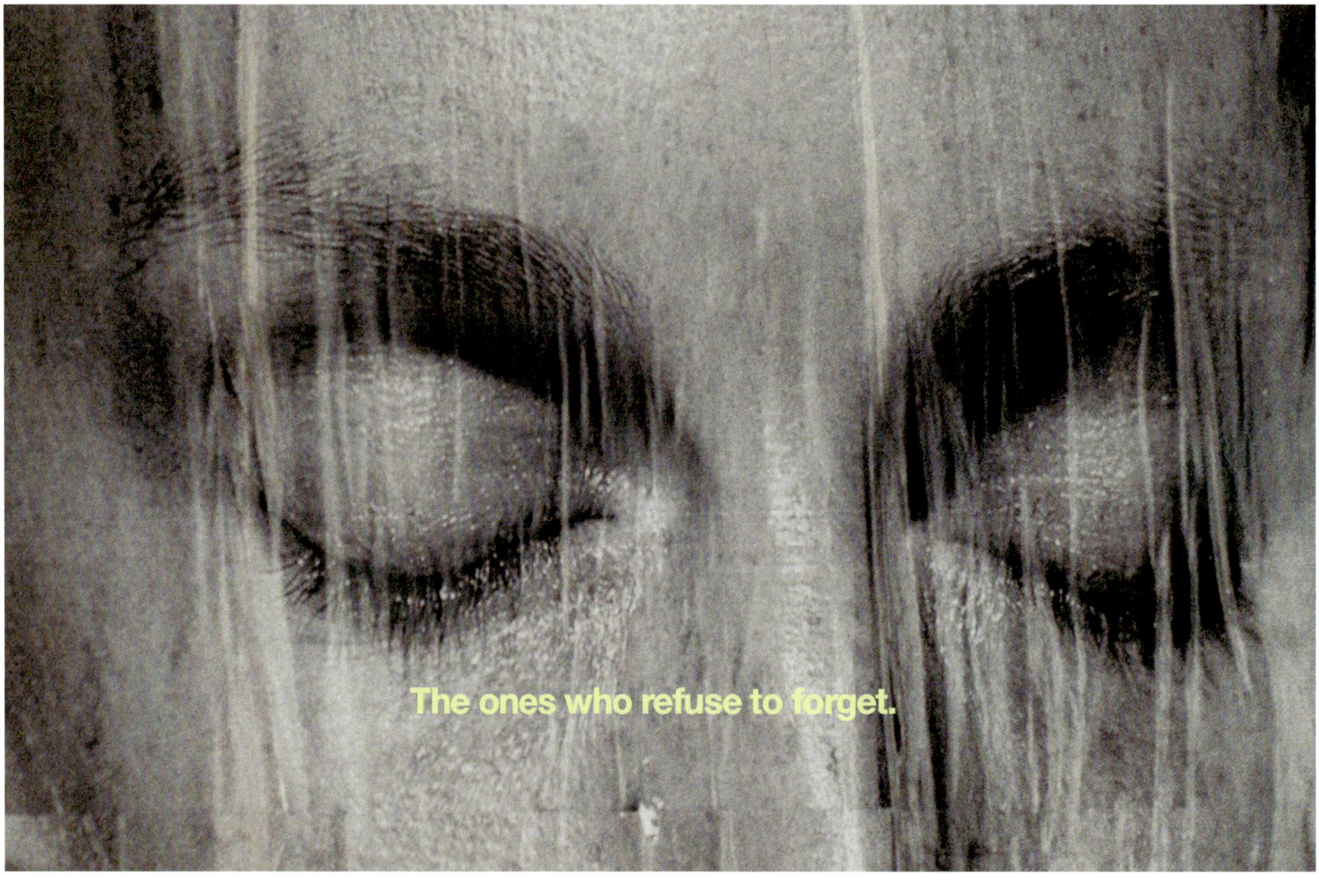

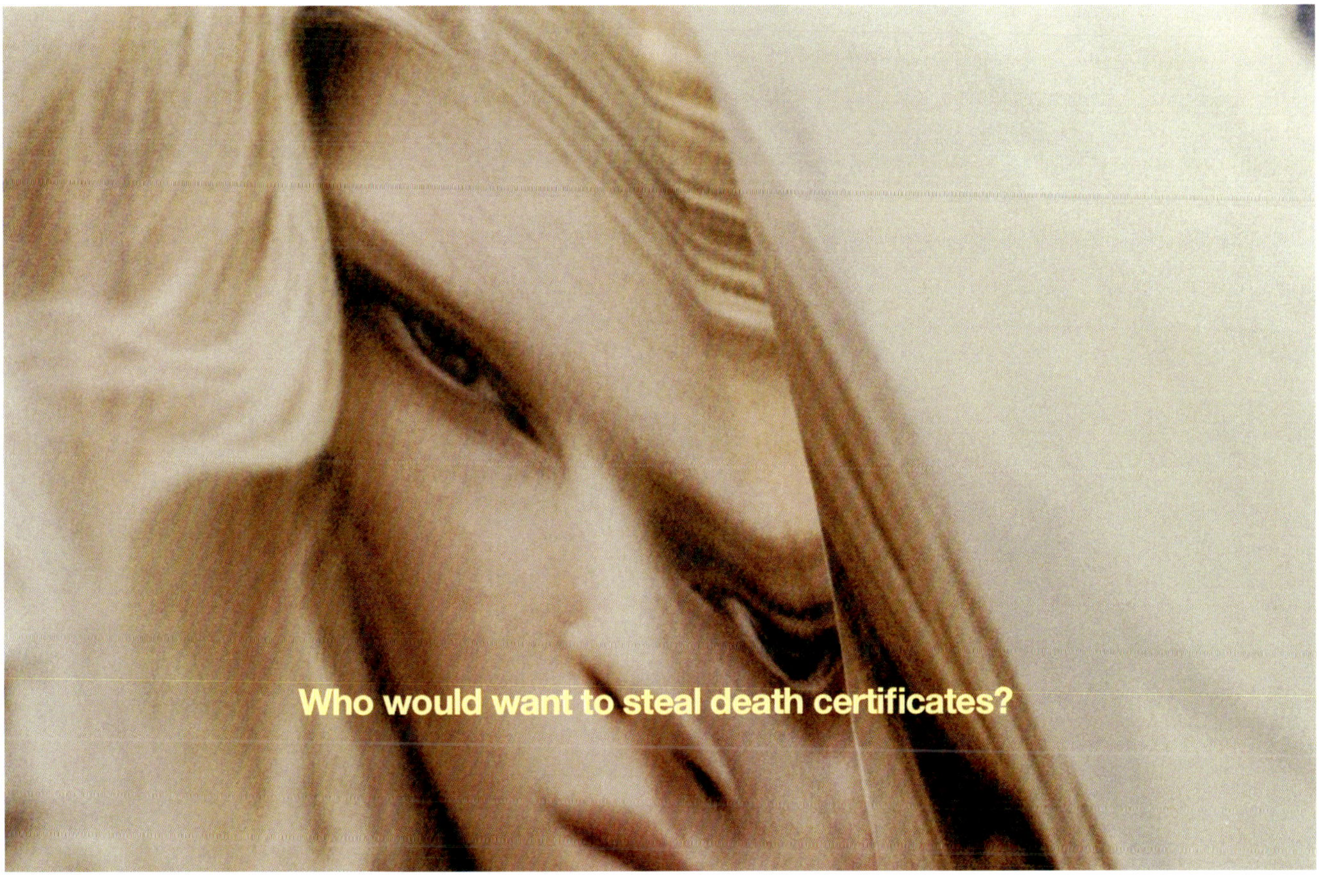

Who would want to steal death certificates?

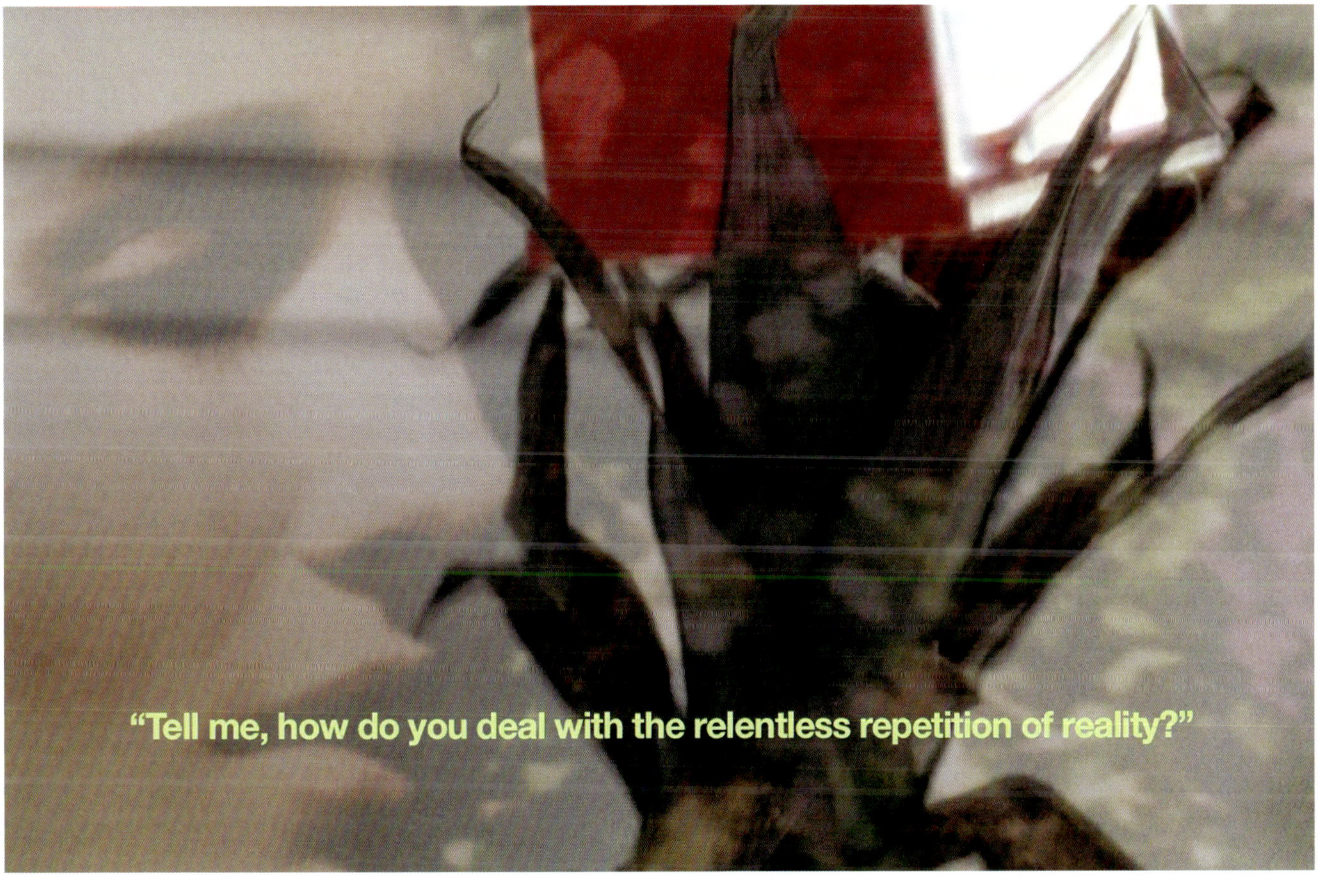

"Tell me, how do you deal with the relentless repetition of reality?"

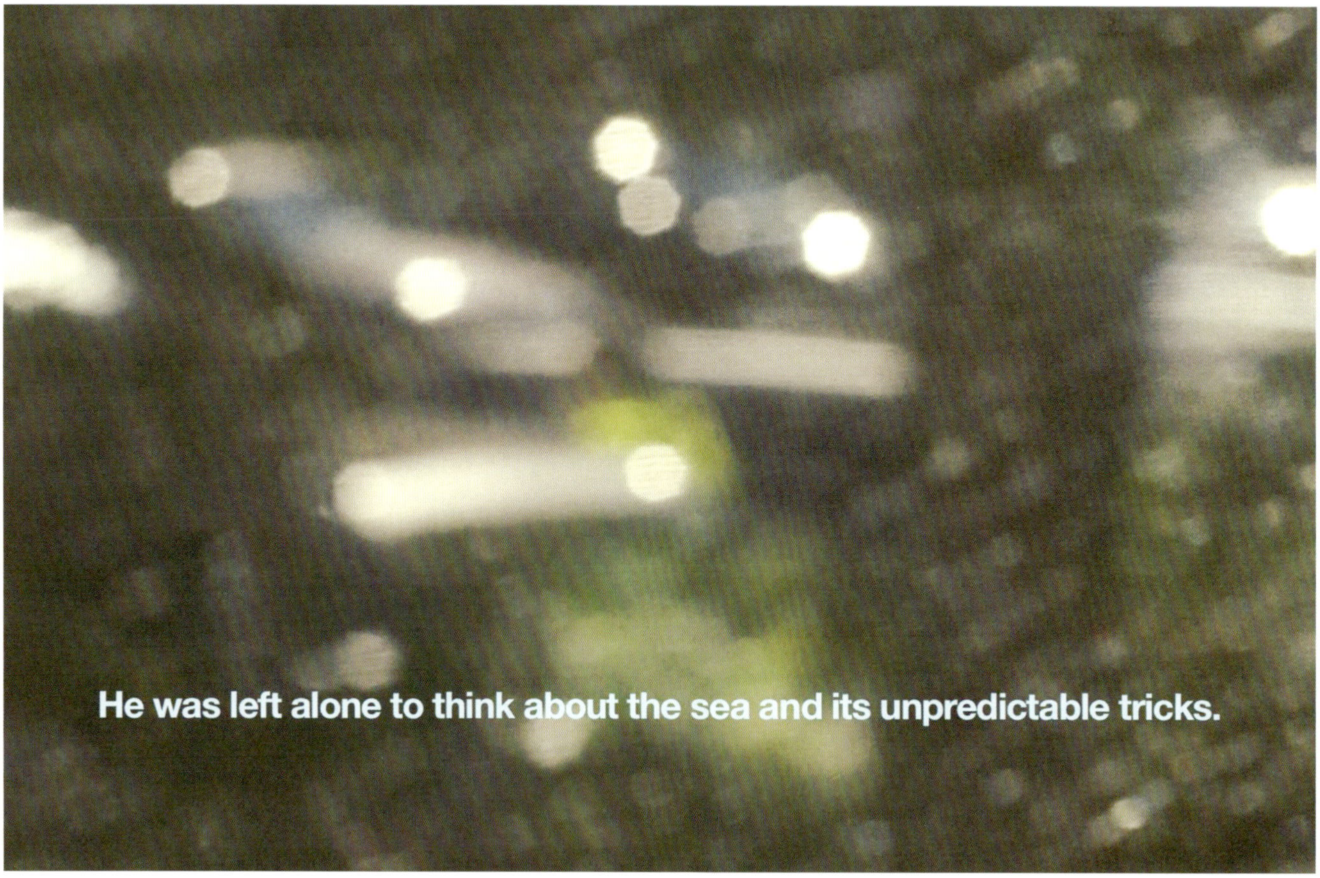

He was left alone to think about the sea and its unpredictable tricks.

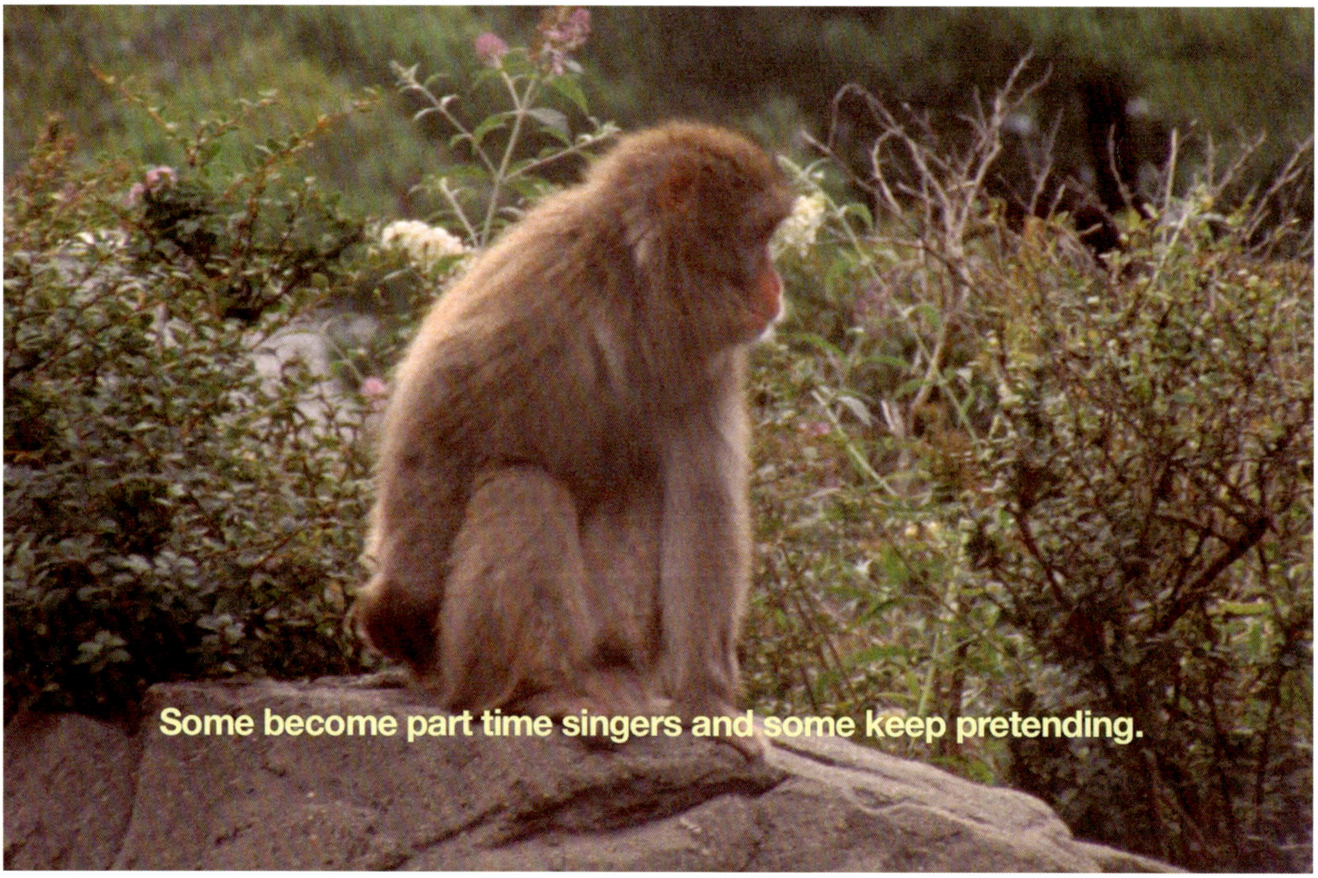

Some become part time singers and some keep pretending.

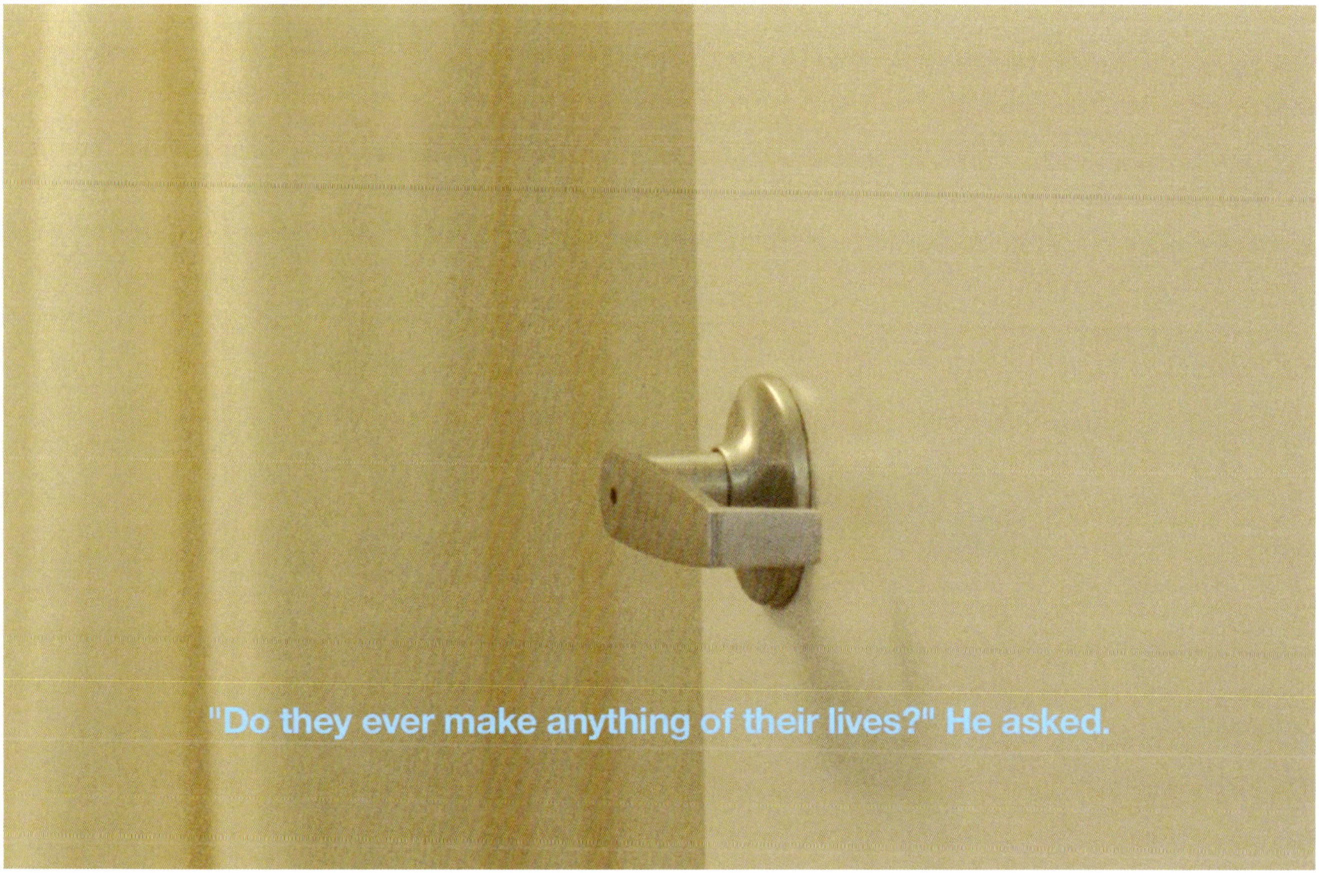

"Do they ever make anything of their lives?" He asked.

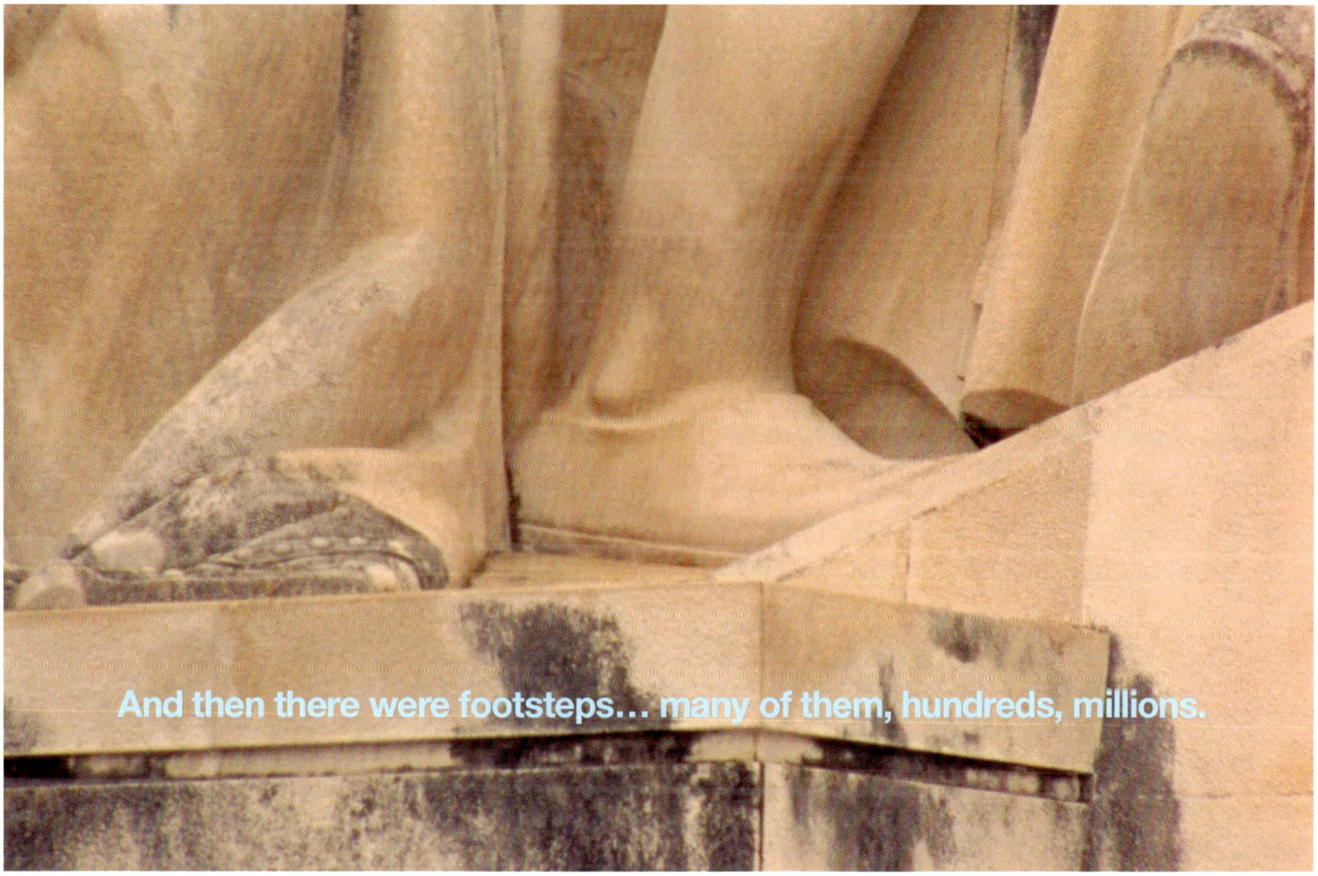

And then there were footsteps… many of them, hundreds, millions.

**WE'RE ALL VICTIMS
OF OUR OWN ADOPTED
FANTASIES HERE
(REPRISE)**

2017

5 C-PRINTS FROM CHEMICALLY
ALTERED NEGATIVES PRINTED ON
METALLIC FUJIFLEX PAPER.

150 X 147 CM OVERALL

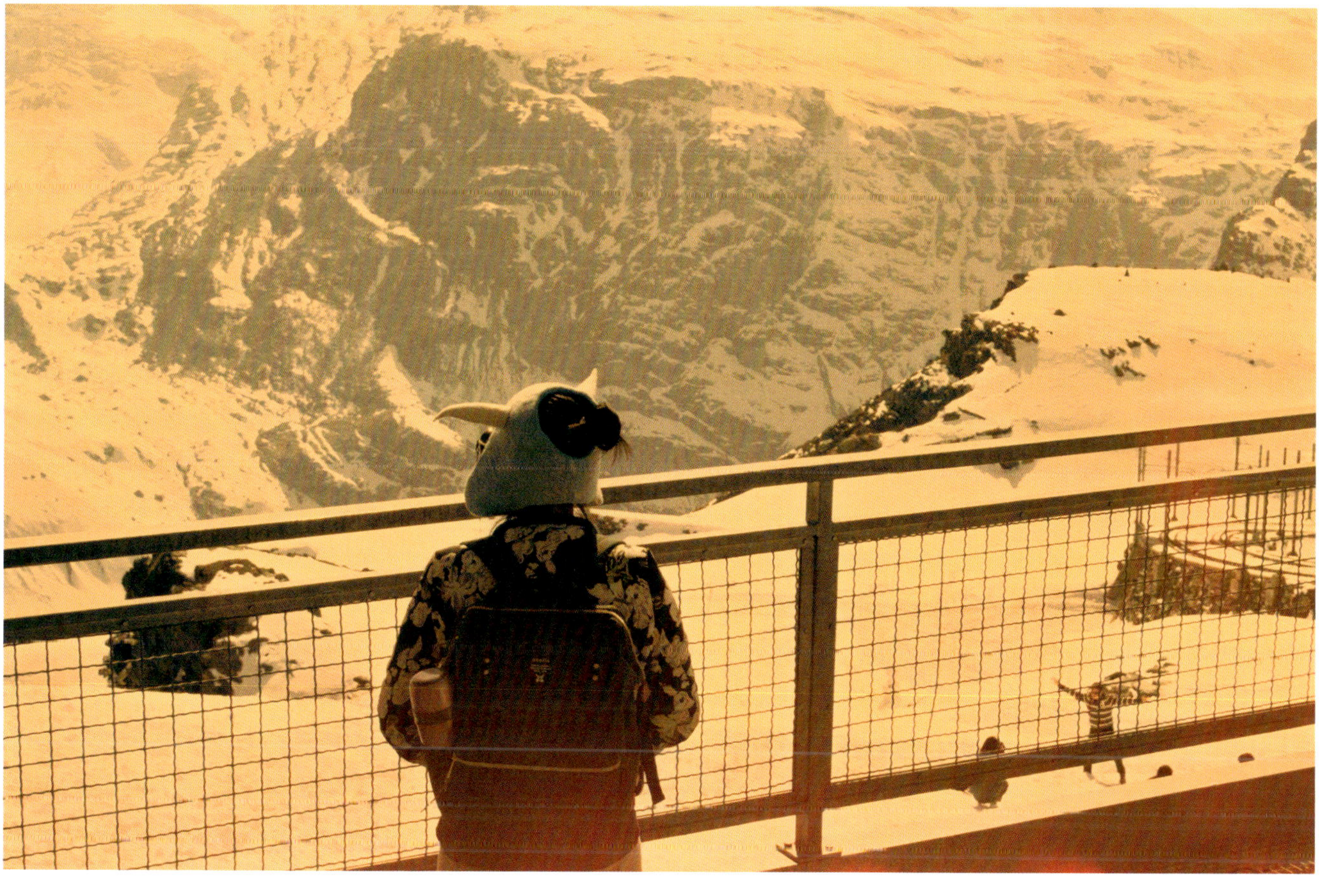

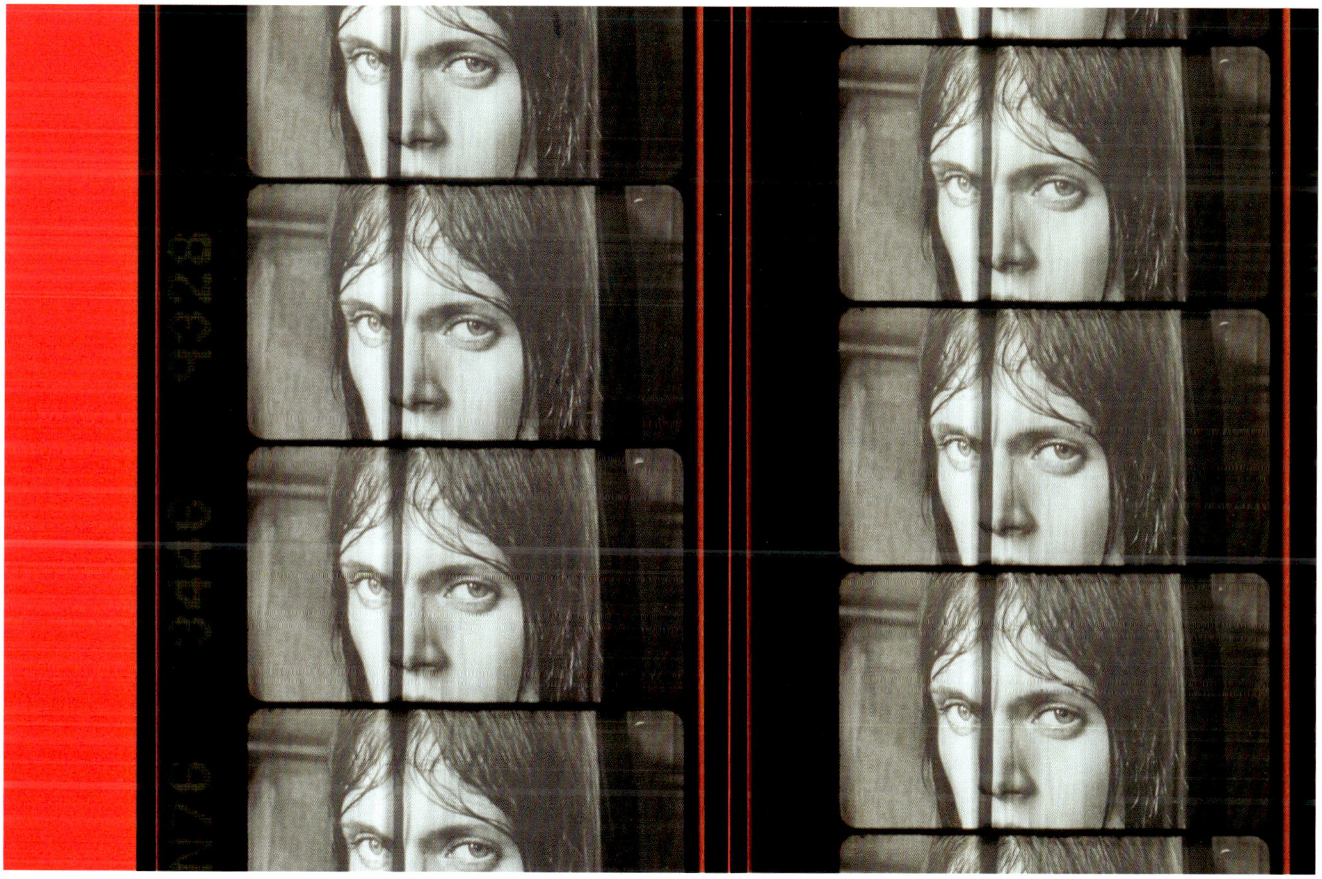

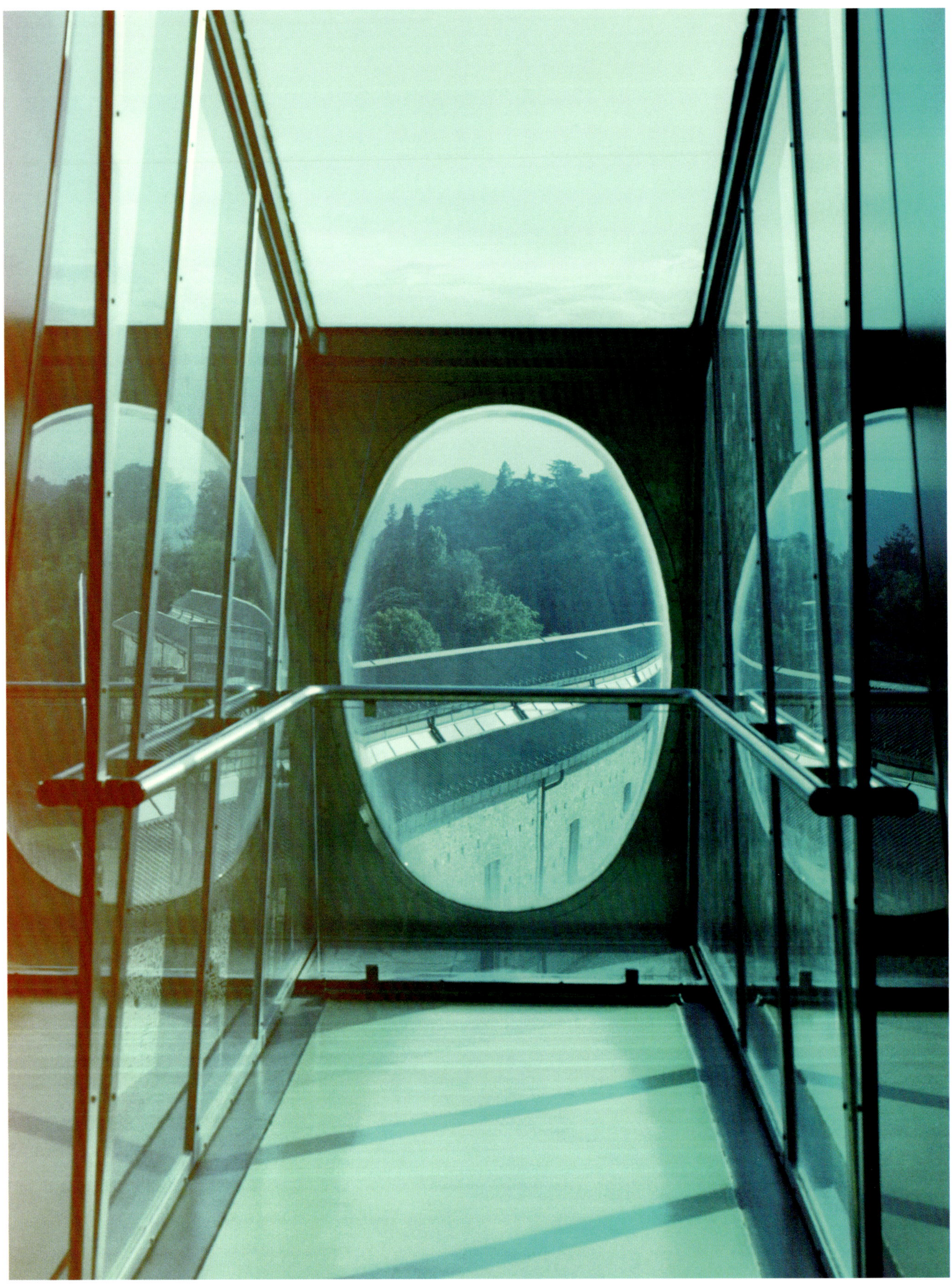

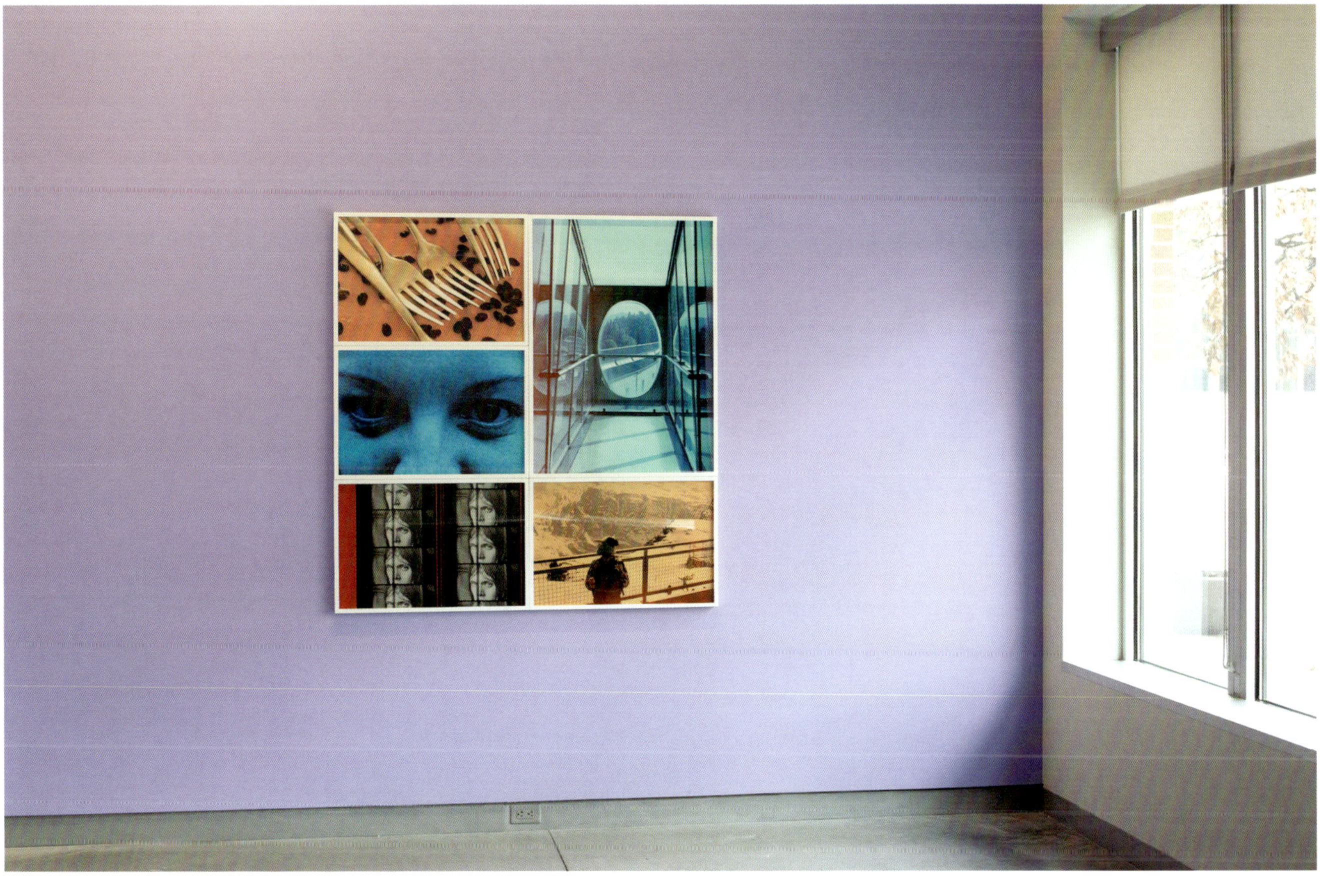

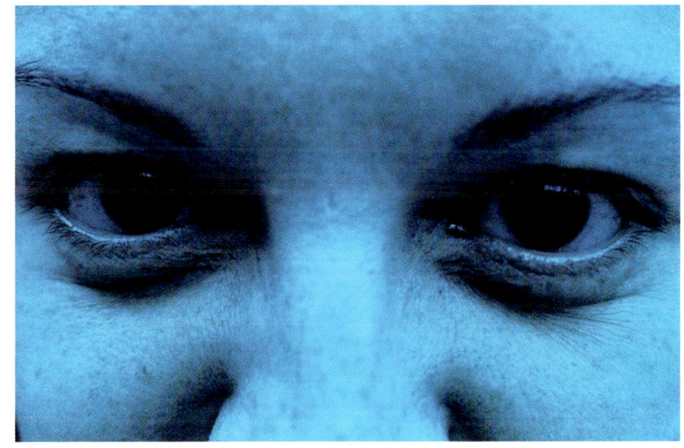

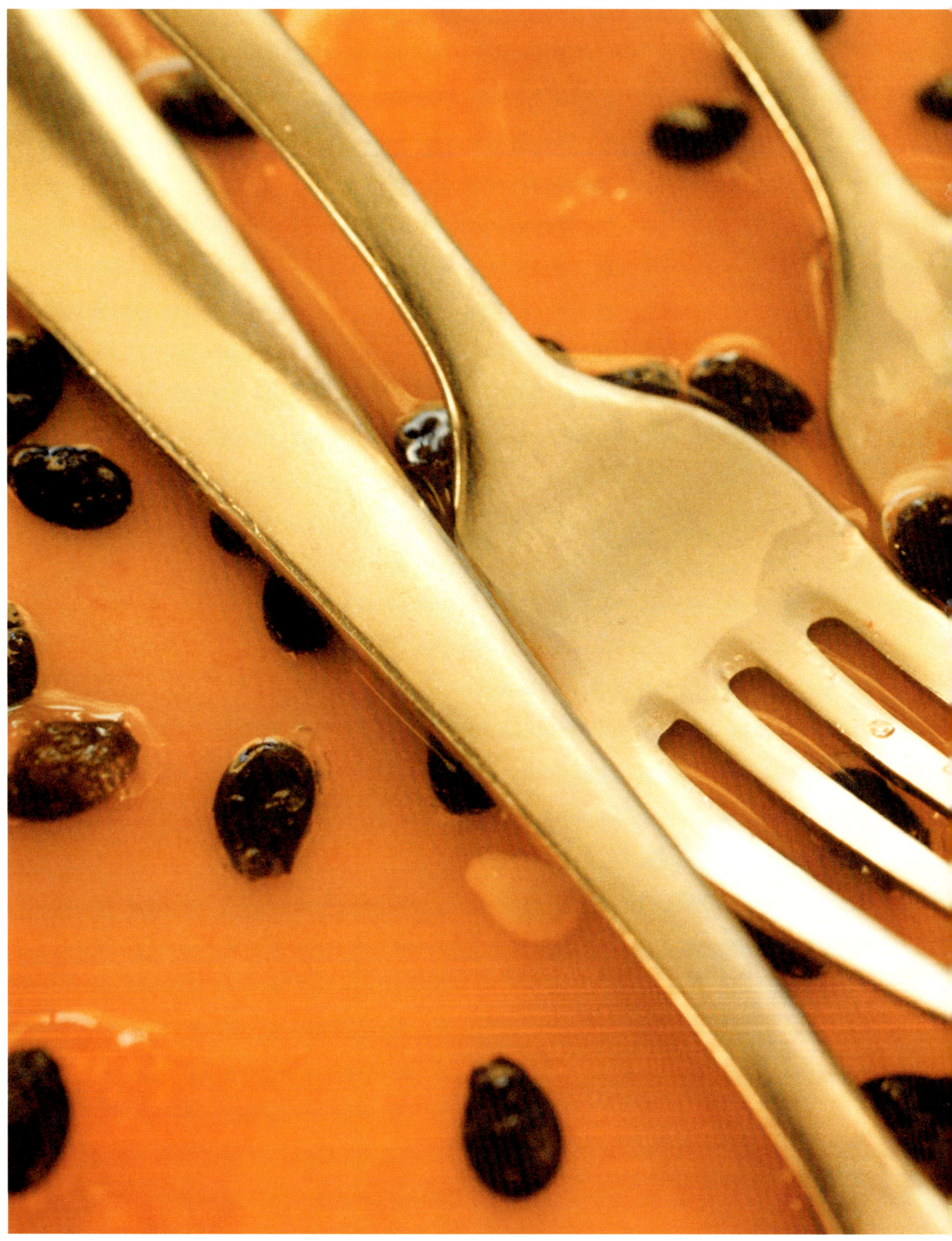

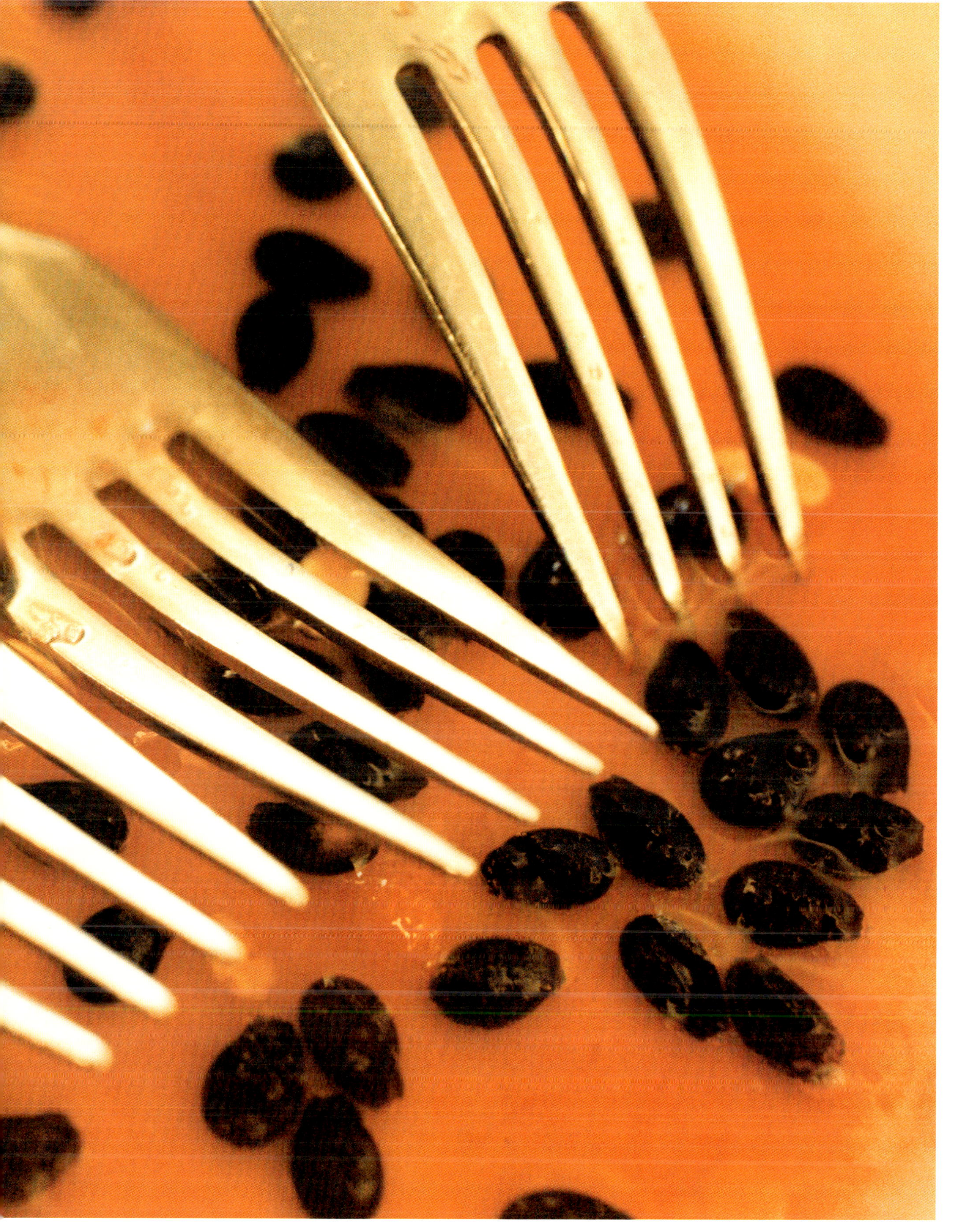

CRYSTAL BALL

2013

DOUBLE SUPER 8 FILM
TRANSFERRED TO HD VIDEO.

7:00 MINUTES

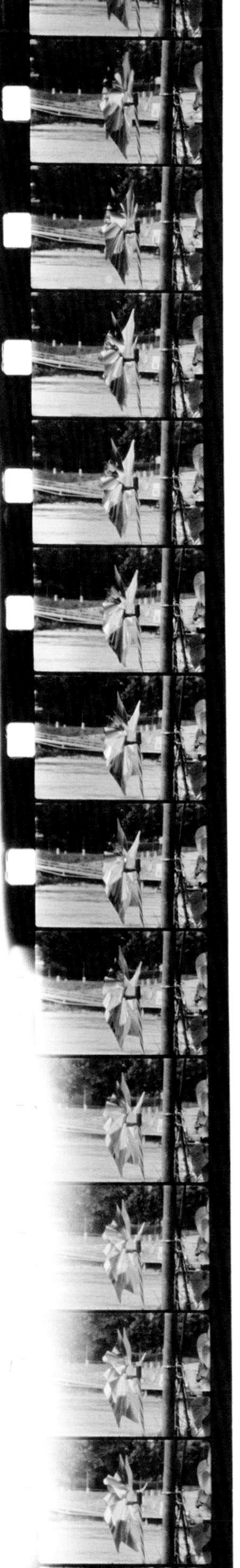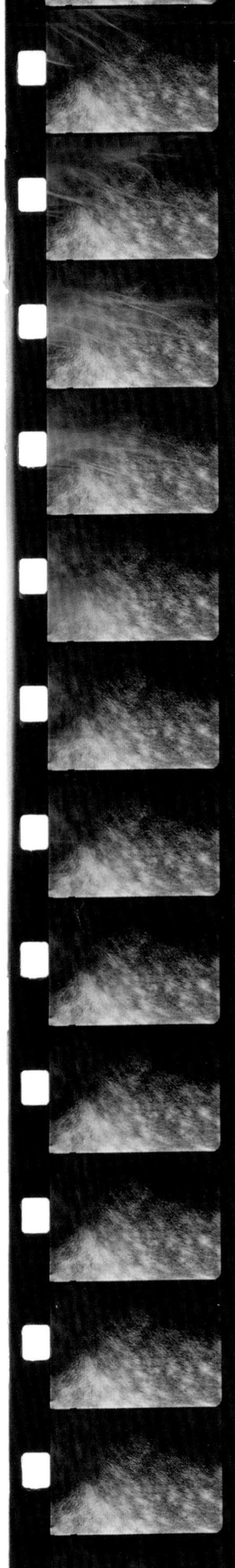

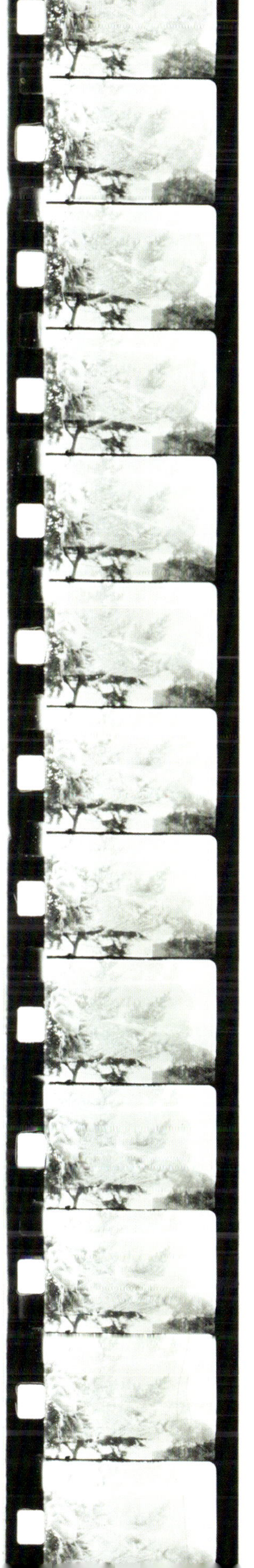
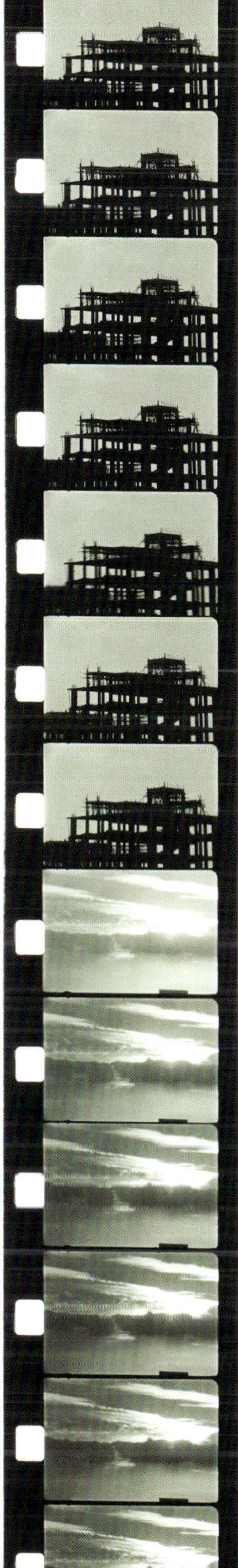
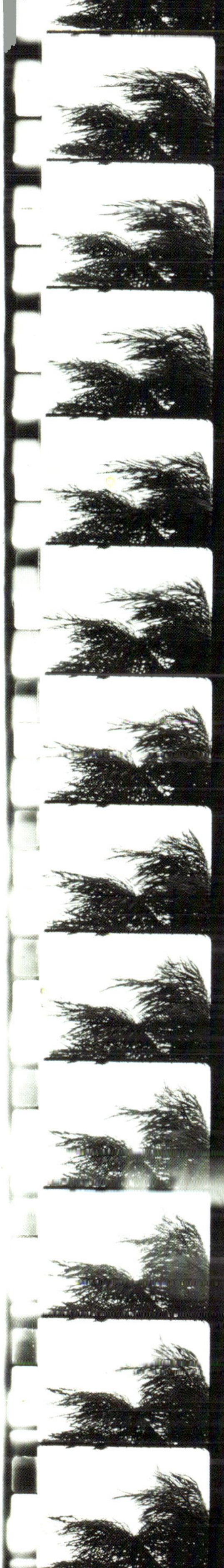
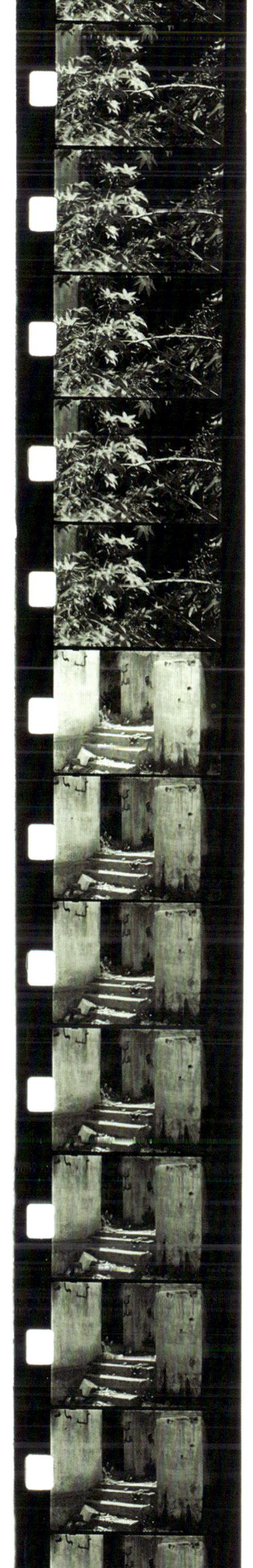

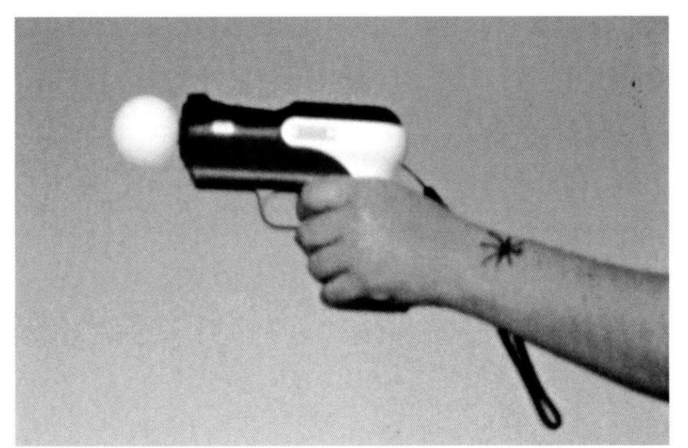 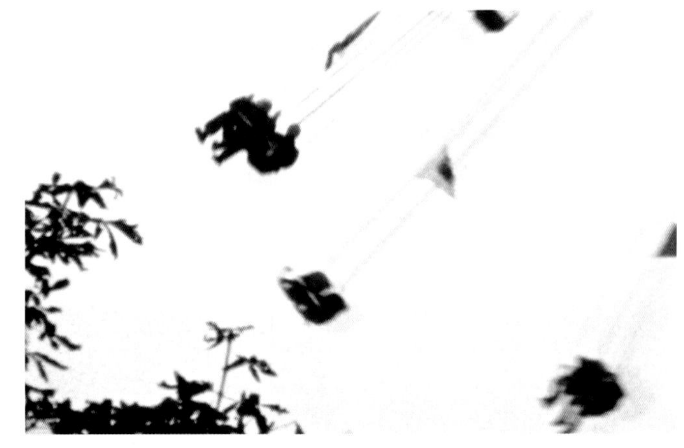

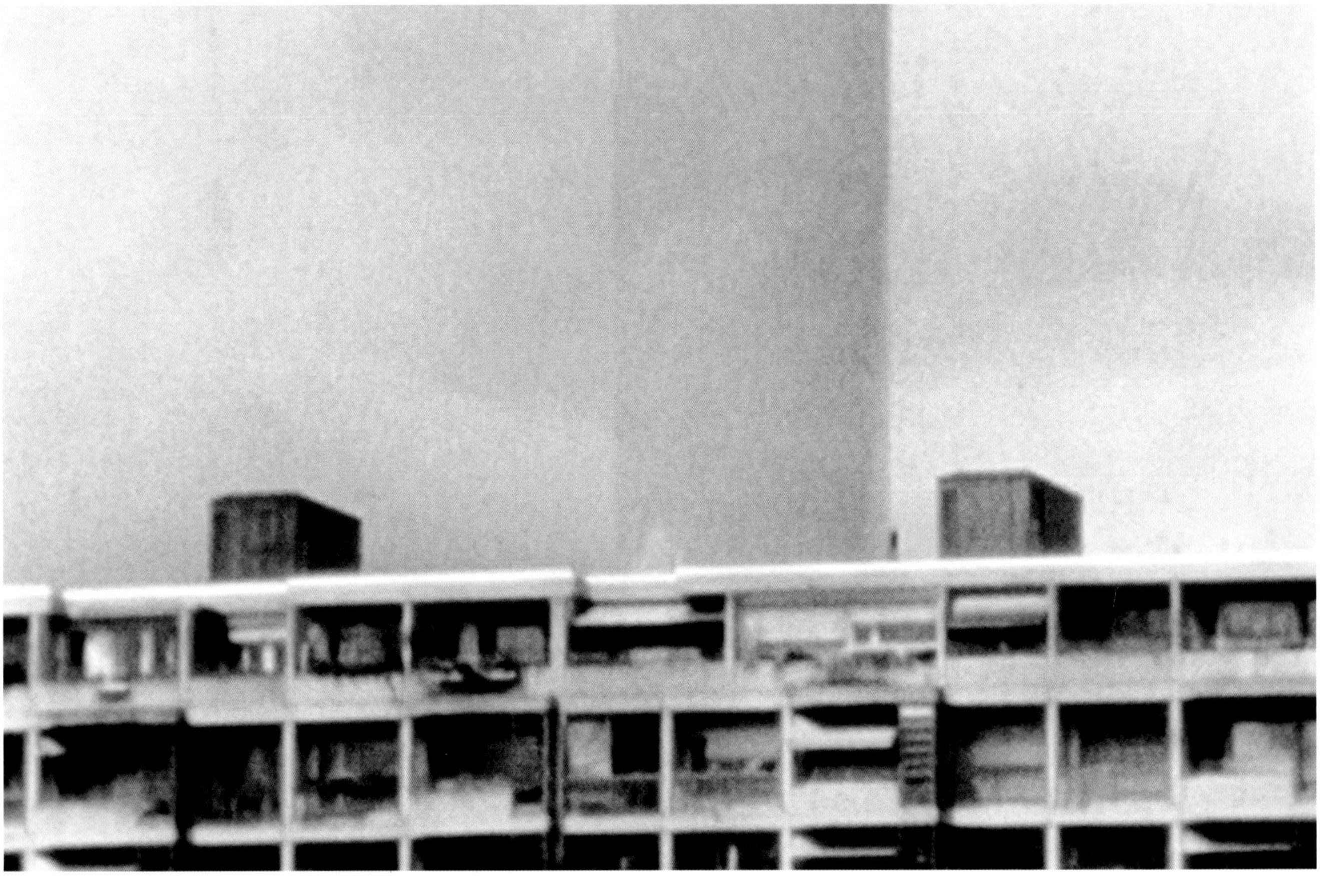

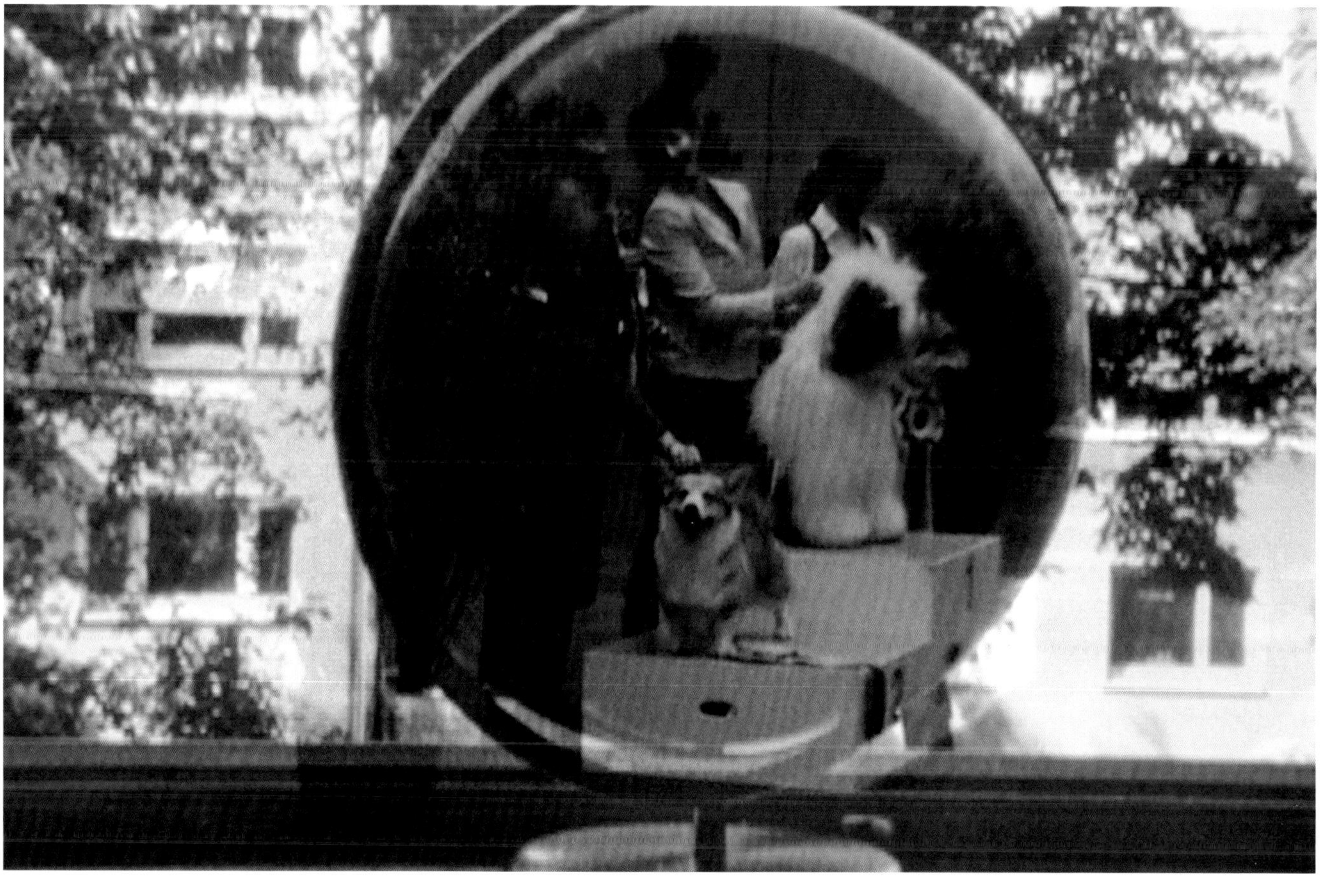

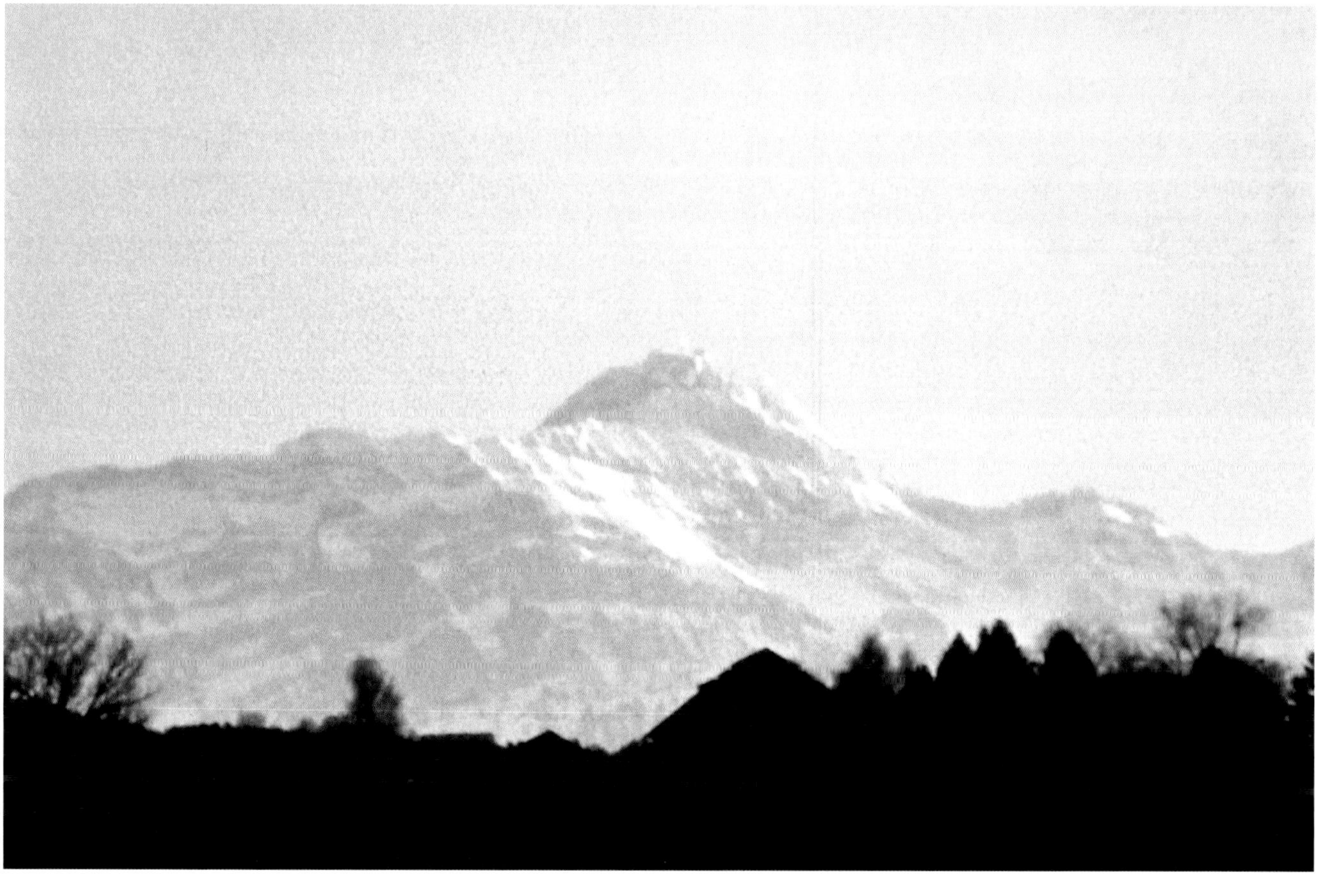

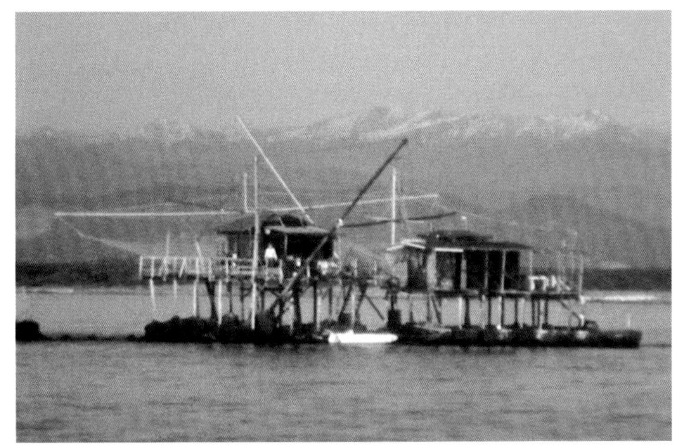

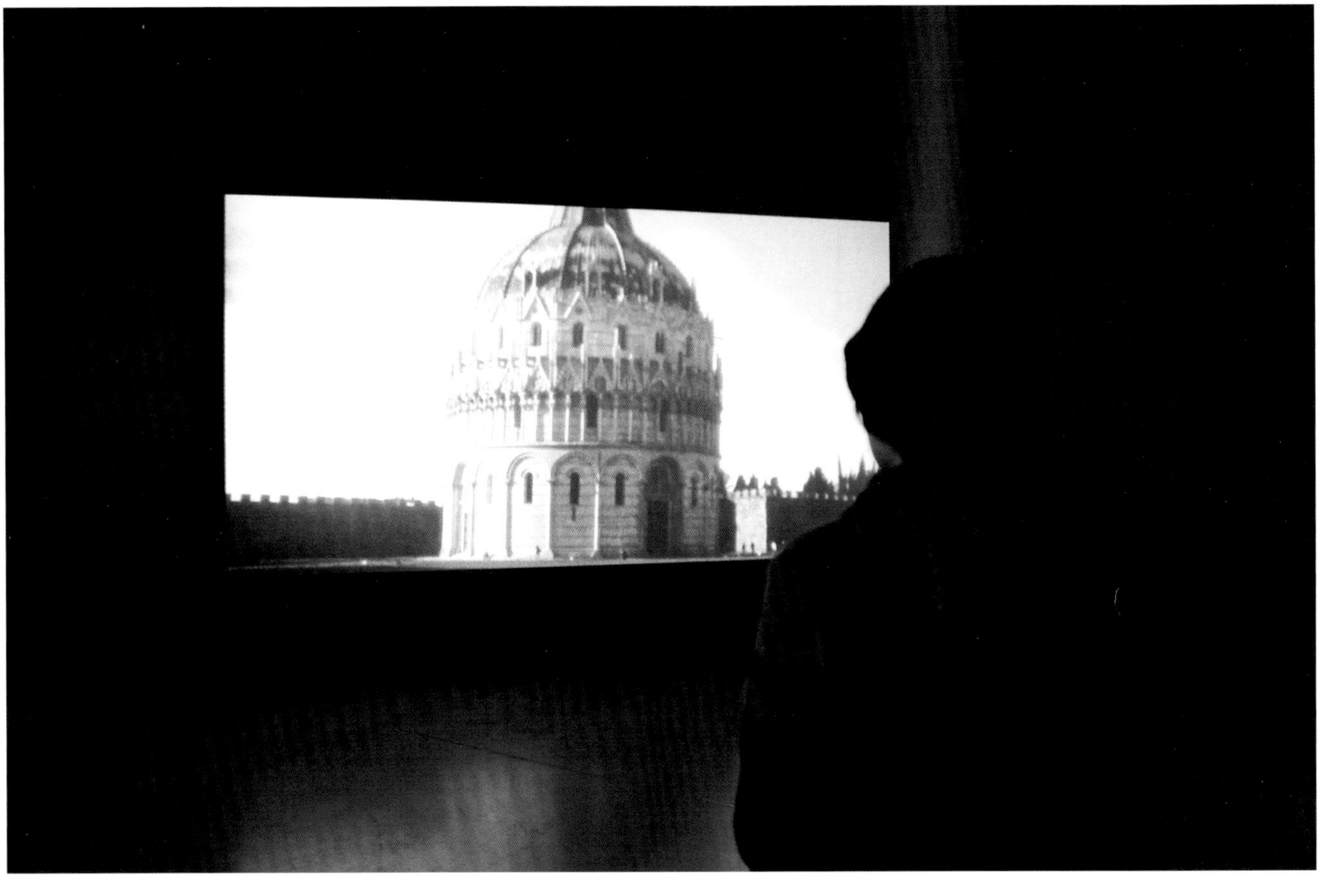

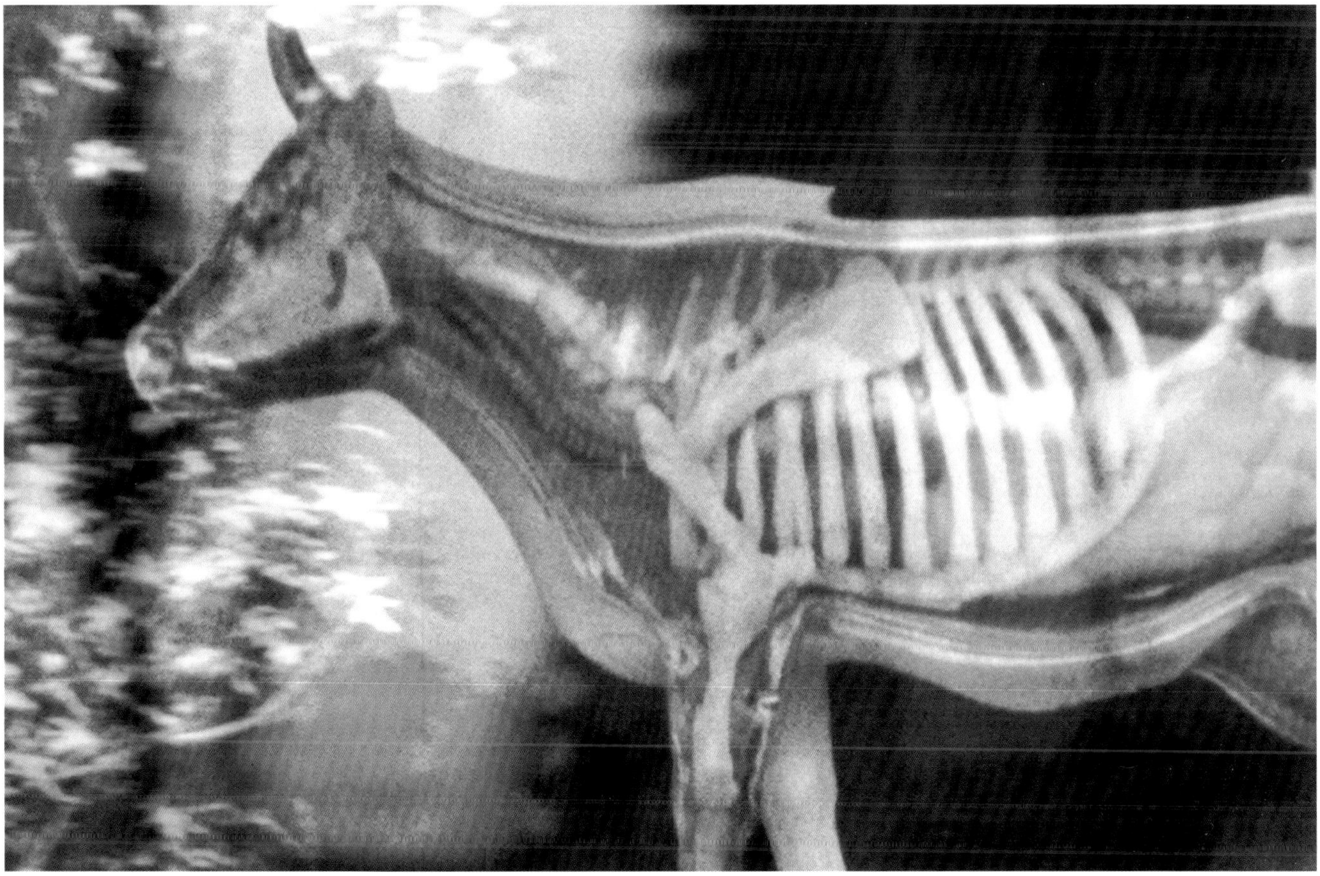

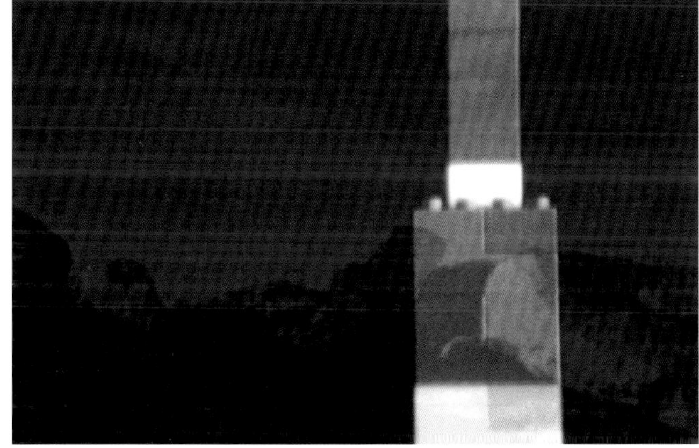

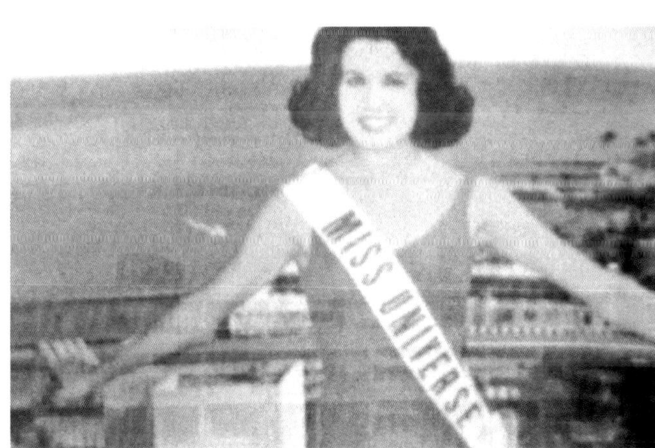
MISS UNIVERSE

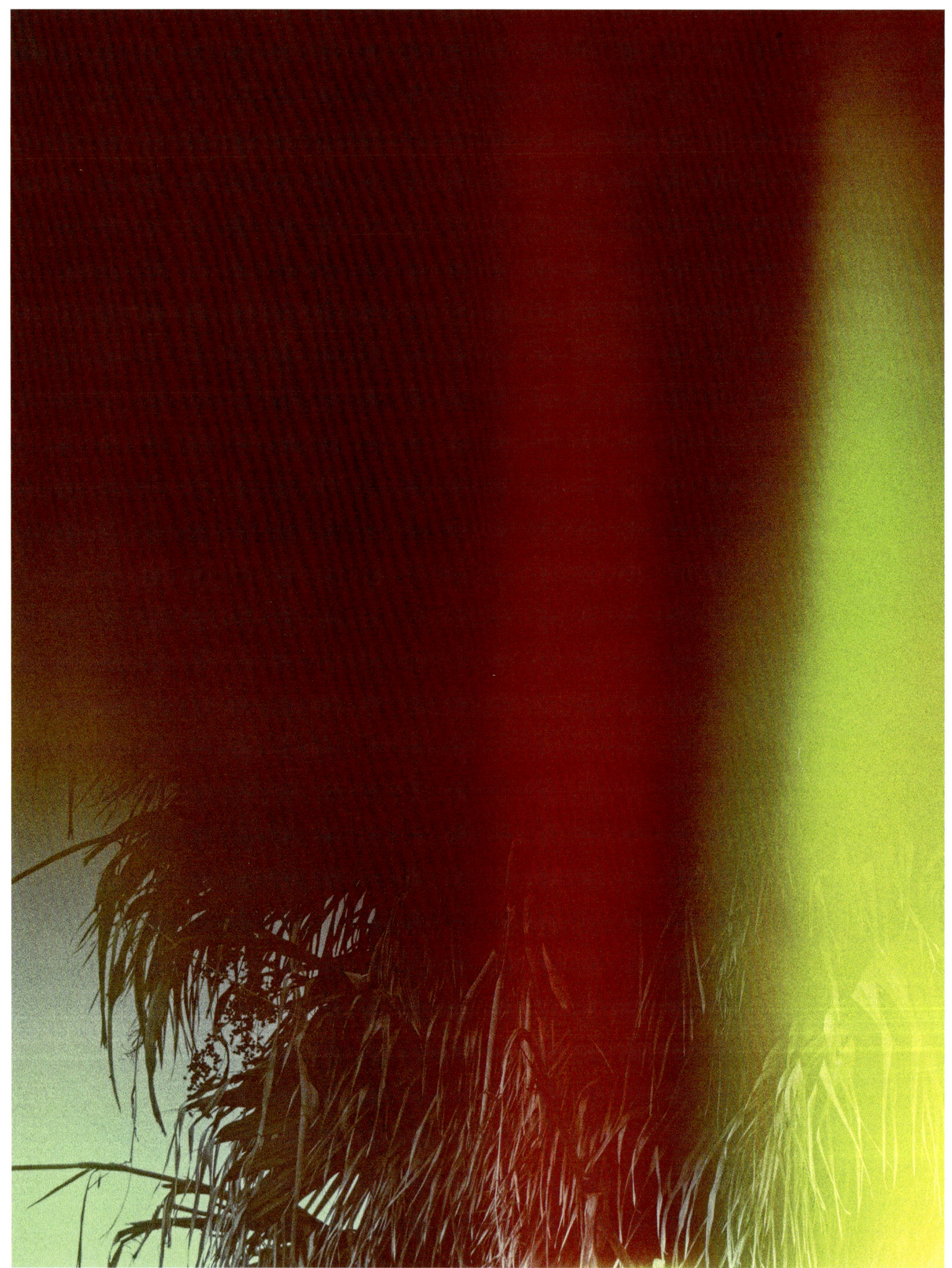

I AM THE IMMIGRANT WHO EXPERIENCED MORE ON A BOAT THAN IN A LIFETIME OF MATHEMATICAL CONSUMPTION.

An excerpt from the script of *No Shooting Stars*, 2016.

NO SHOOTING STARS

2016

SUPER 16MM AND GIF
ANIMATIONS TRANSFERRED
TO FULL HD VIDEO.

14:25 MINUTES

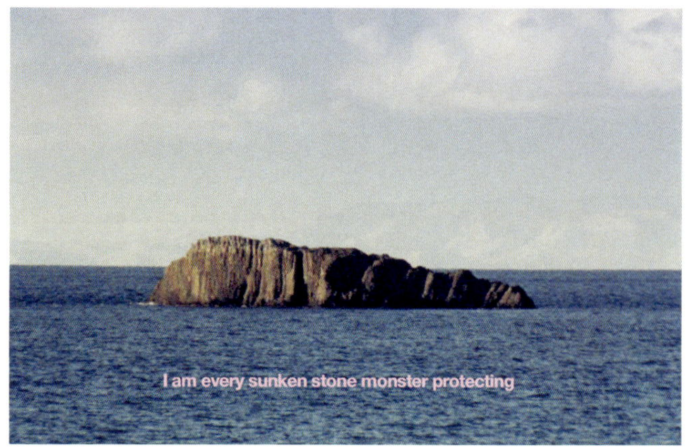

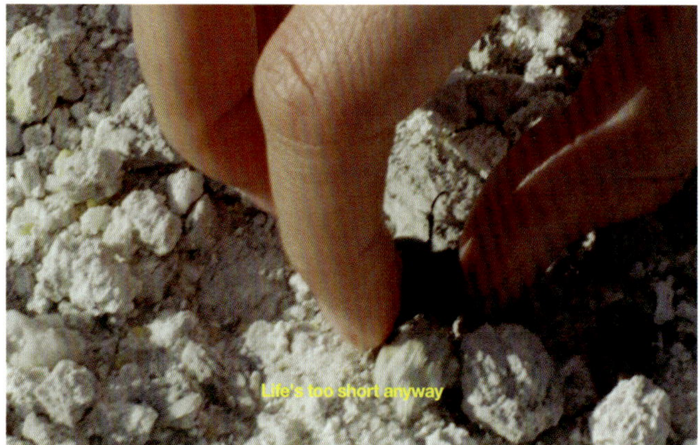

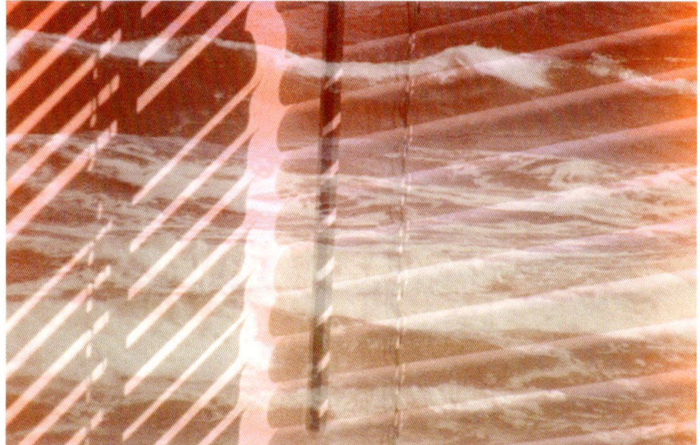

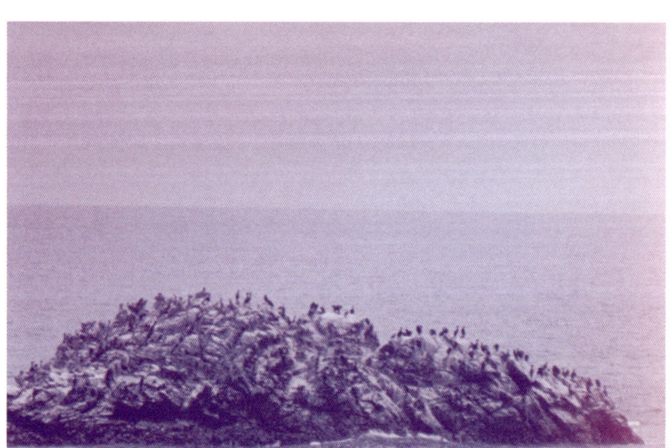

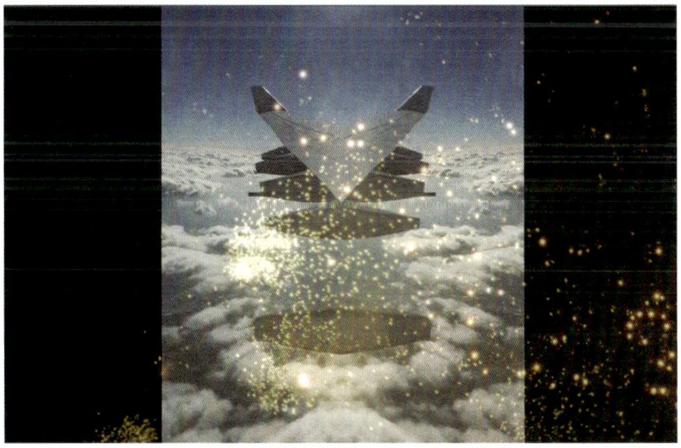

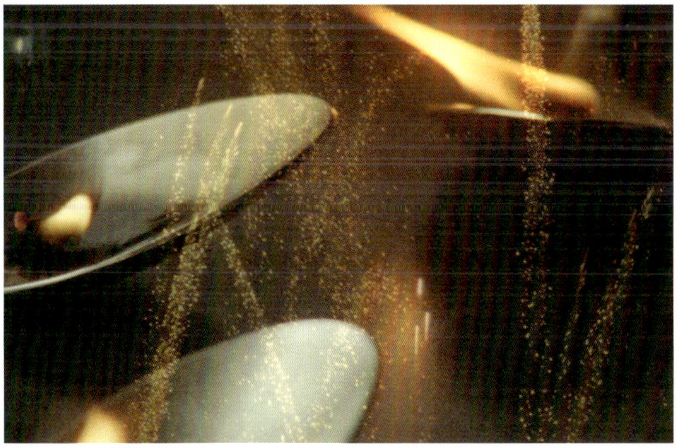

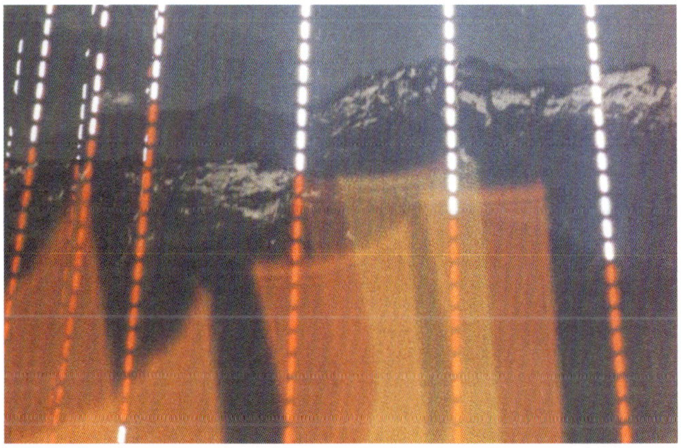

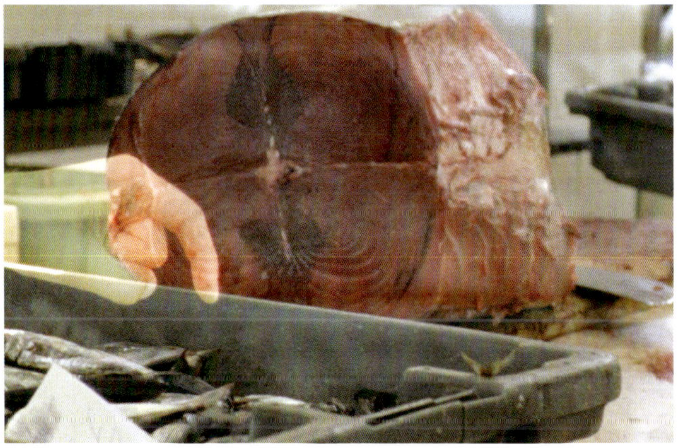

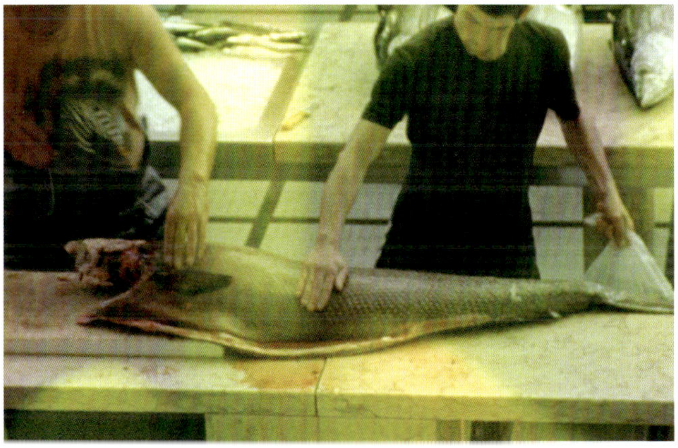

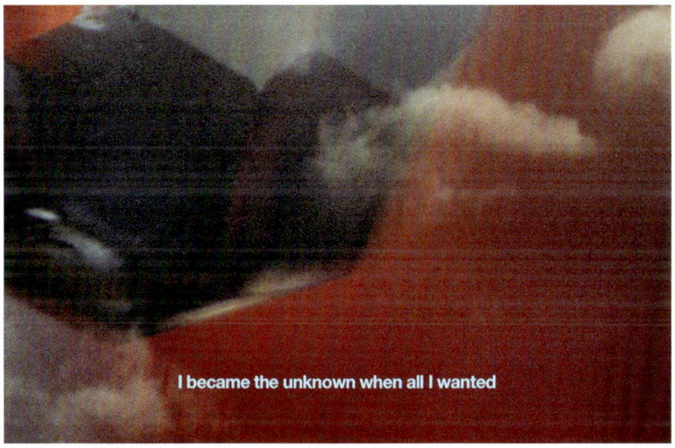

I became the unknown when all I wanted

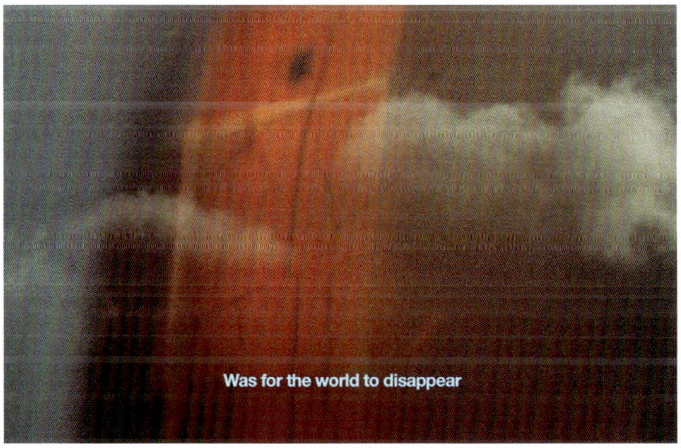

Was for the world to disappear

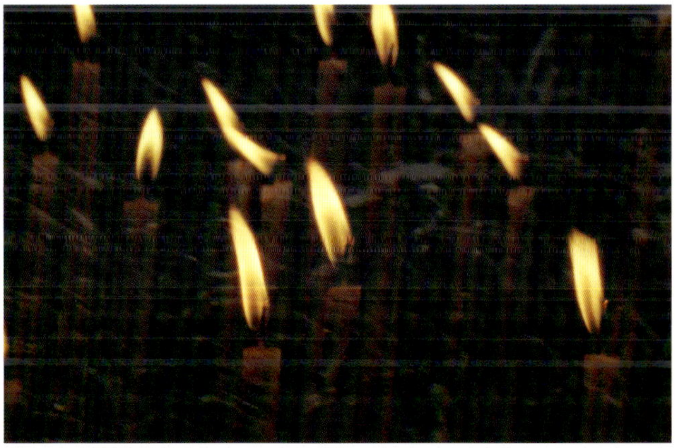

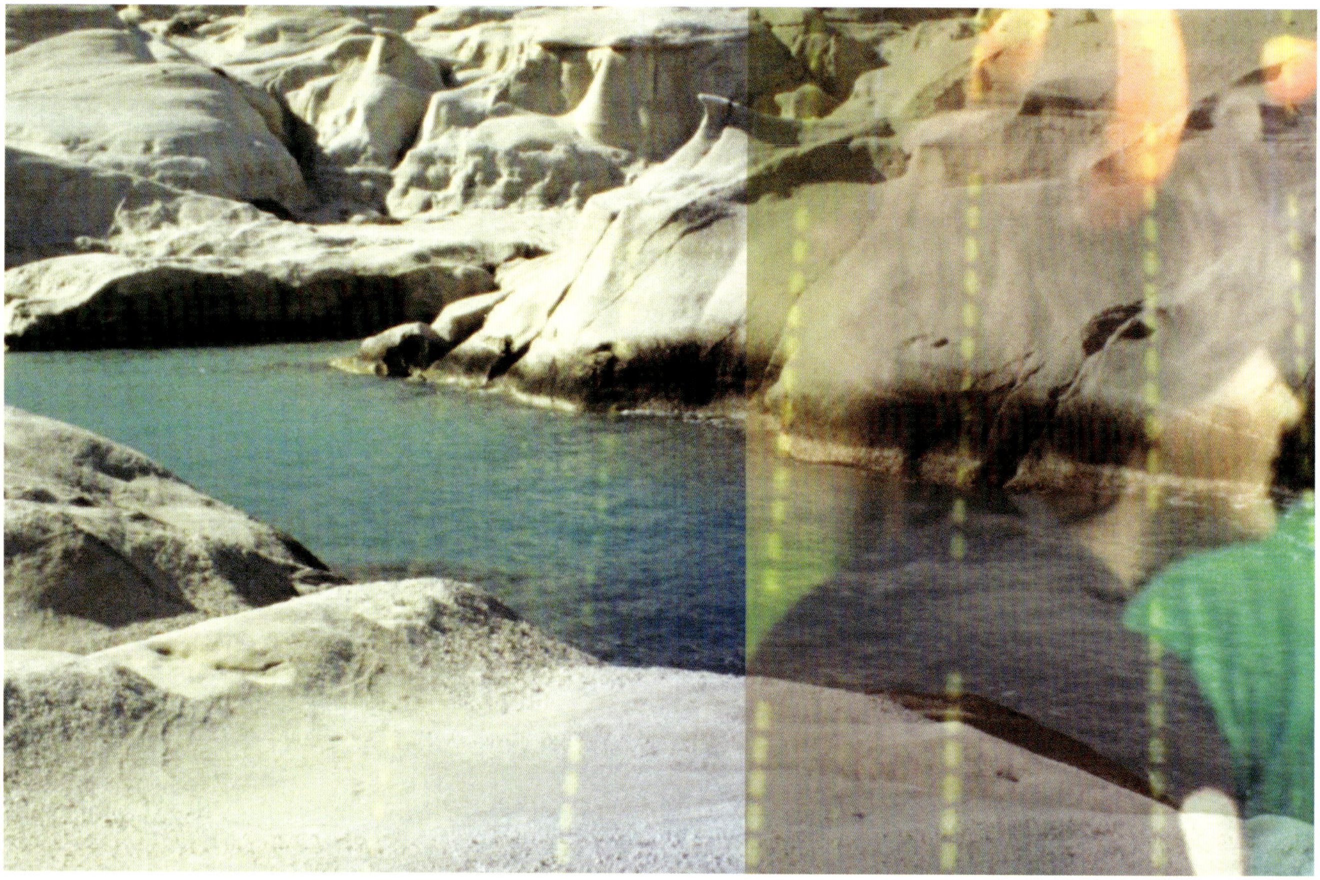

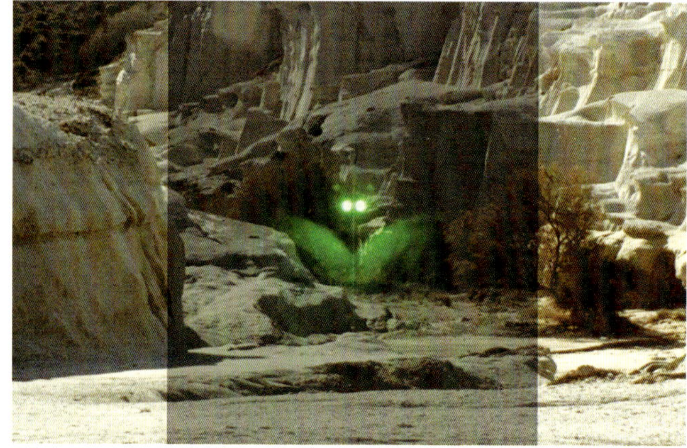

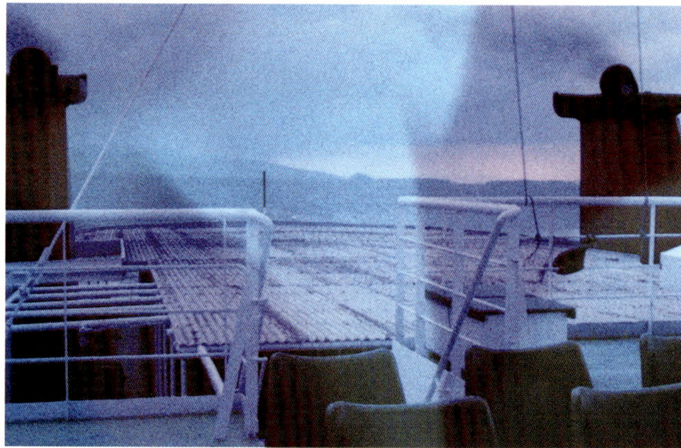

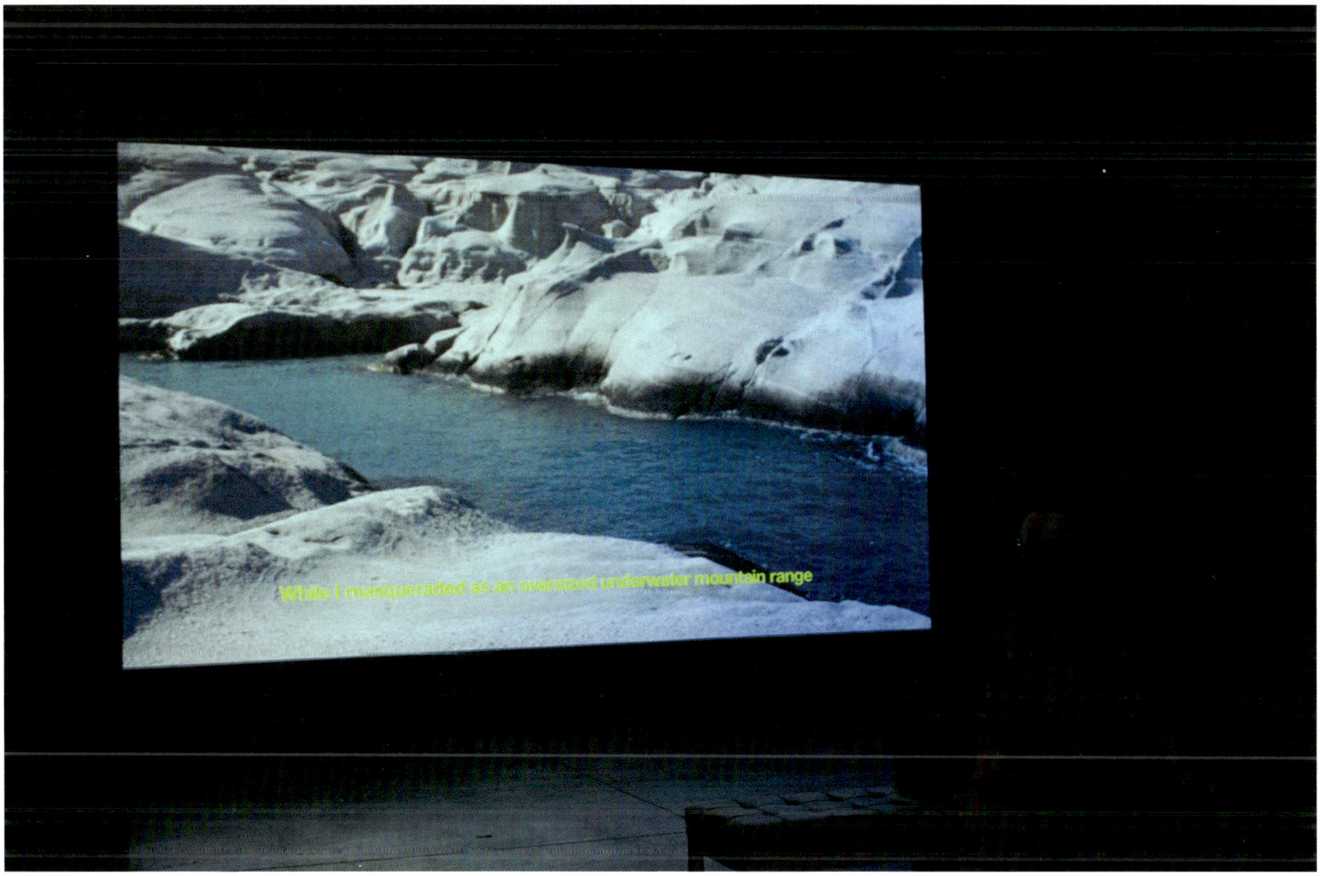

While I masqueraded as an oversized underwater mountain range

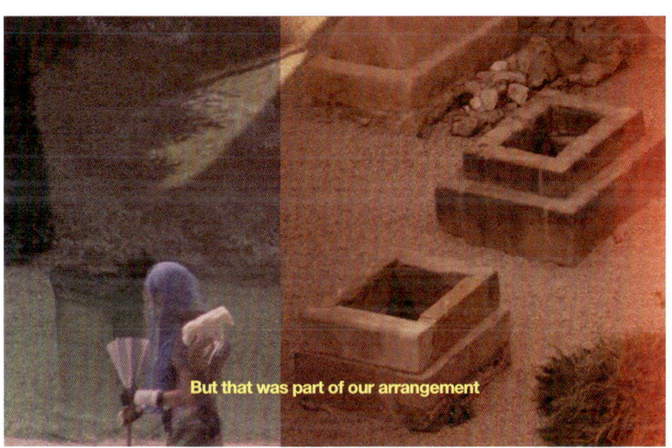
But that was part of our arrangement

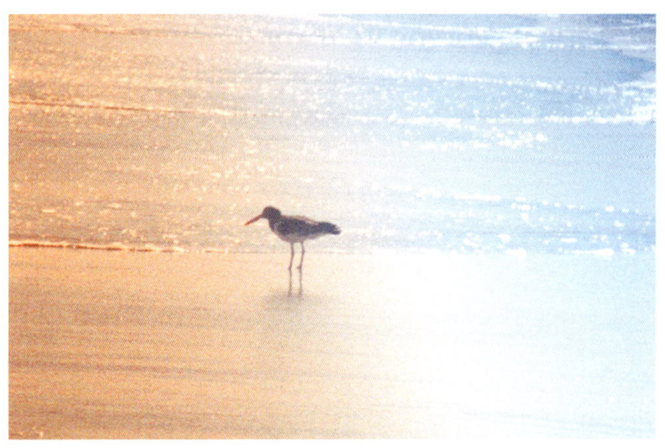

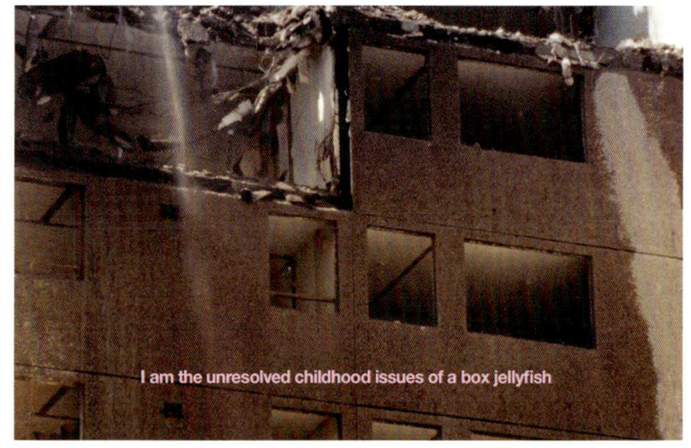
I am the unresolved childhood issues of a box jellyfish

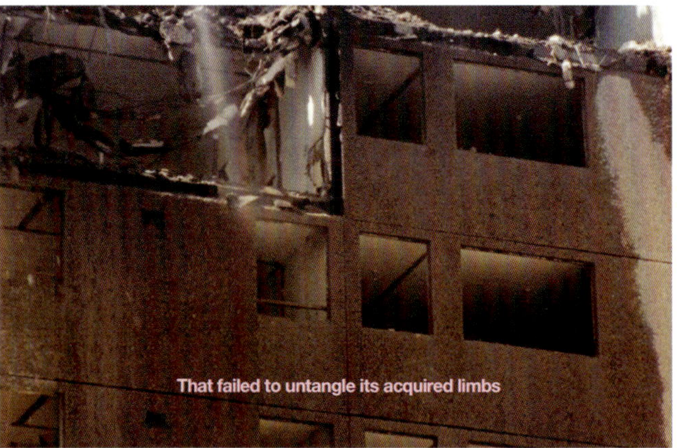
That failed to untangle its acquired limbs

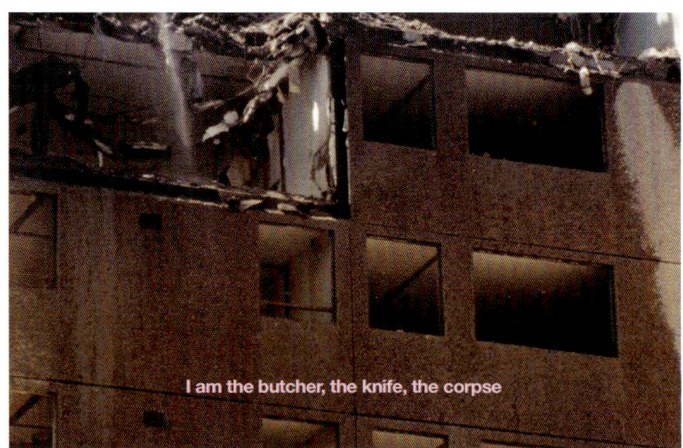
I am the butcher, the knife, the corpse

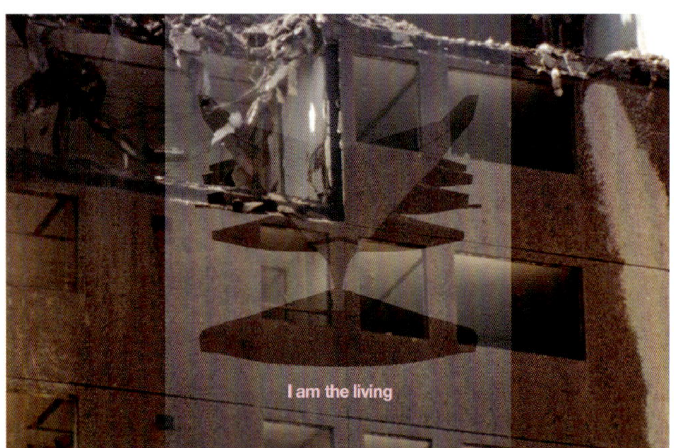
I am the living

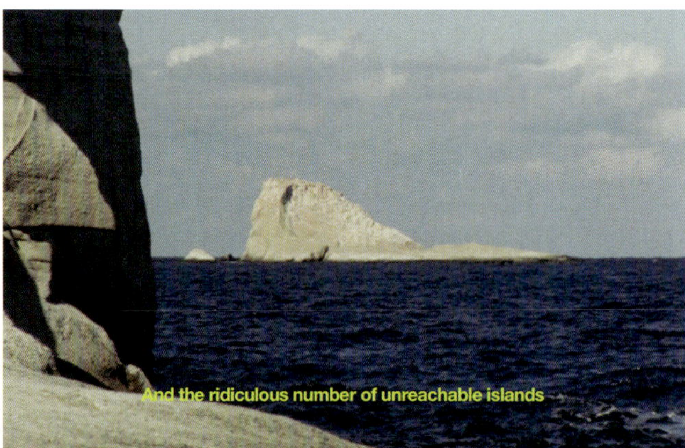
And the ridiculous number of unreachable islands

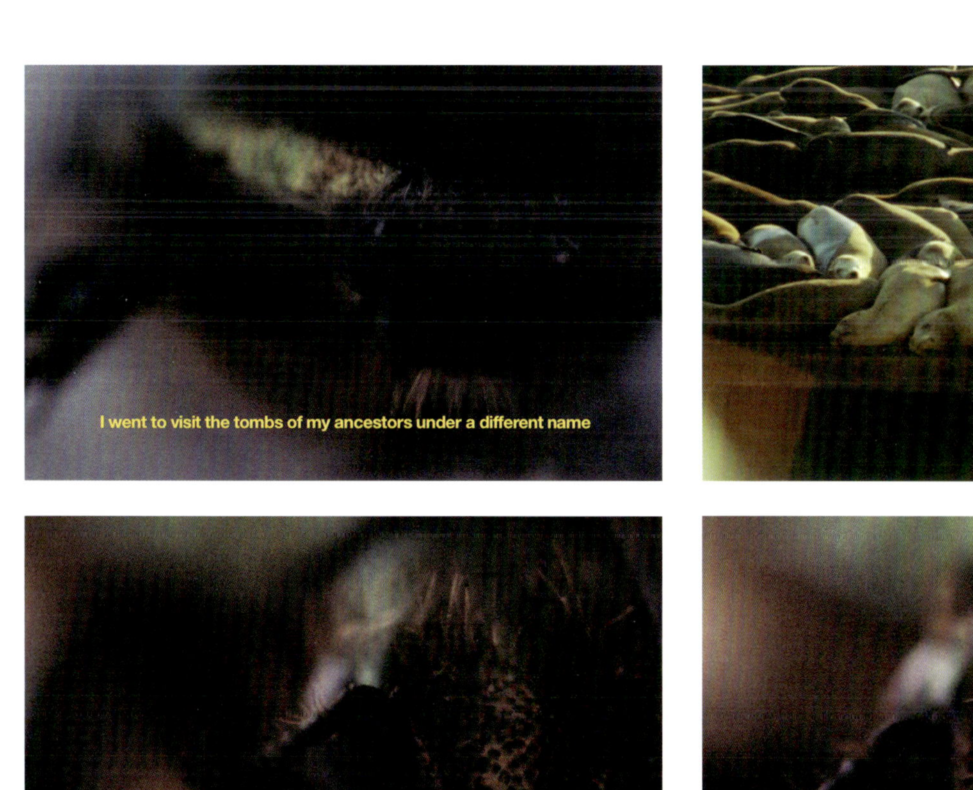
I went to visit the tombs of my ancestors under a different name

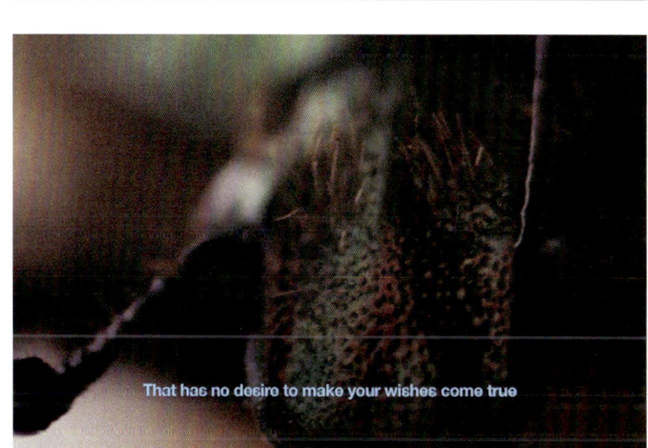

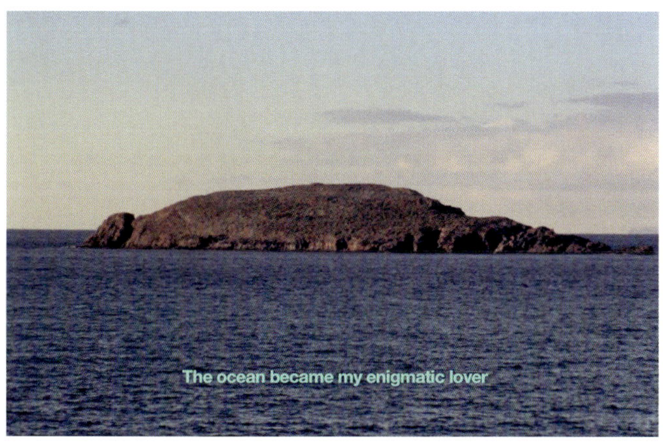
Down here there is another existence

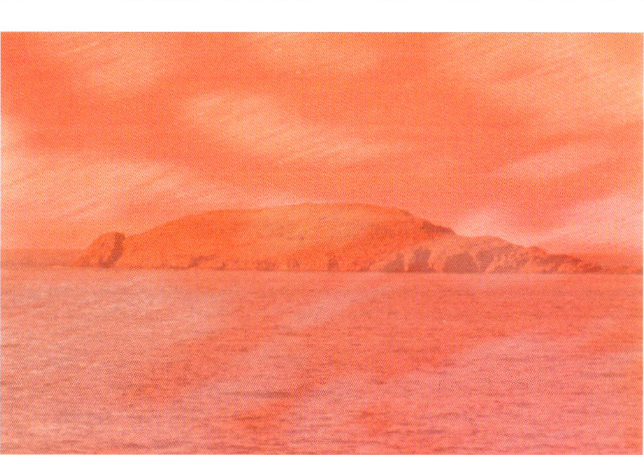
That has no desire to make your wishes come true

The ocean became my enigmatic lover

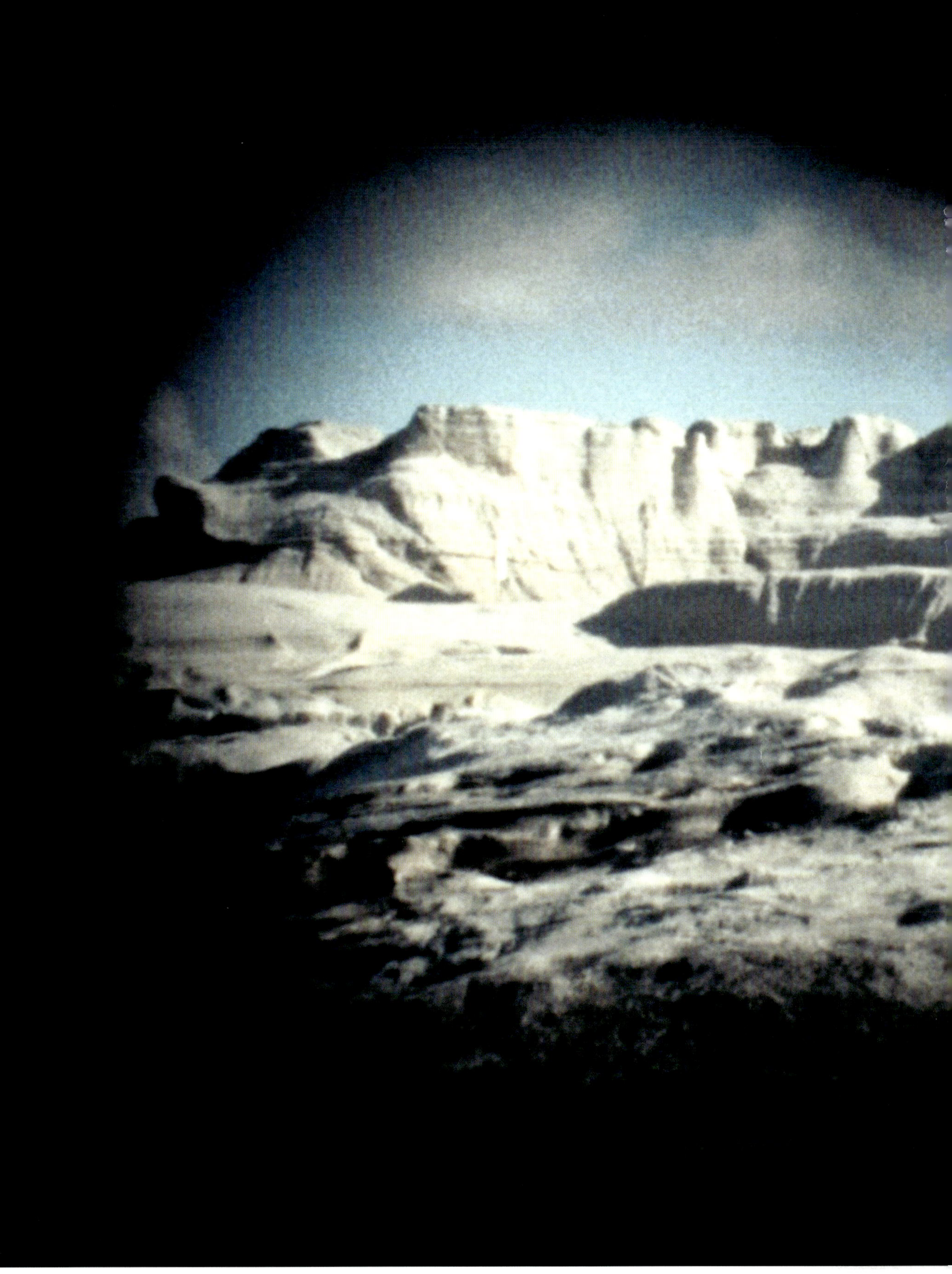

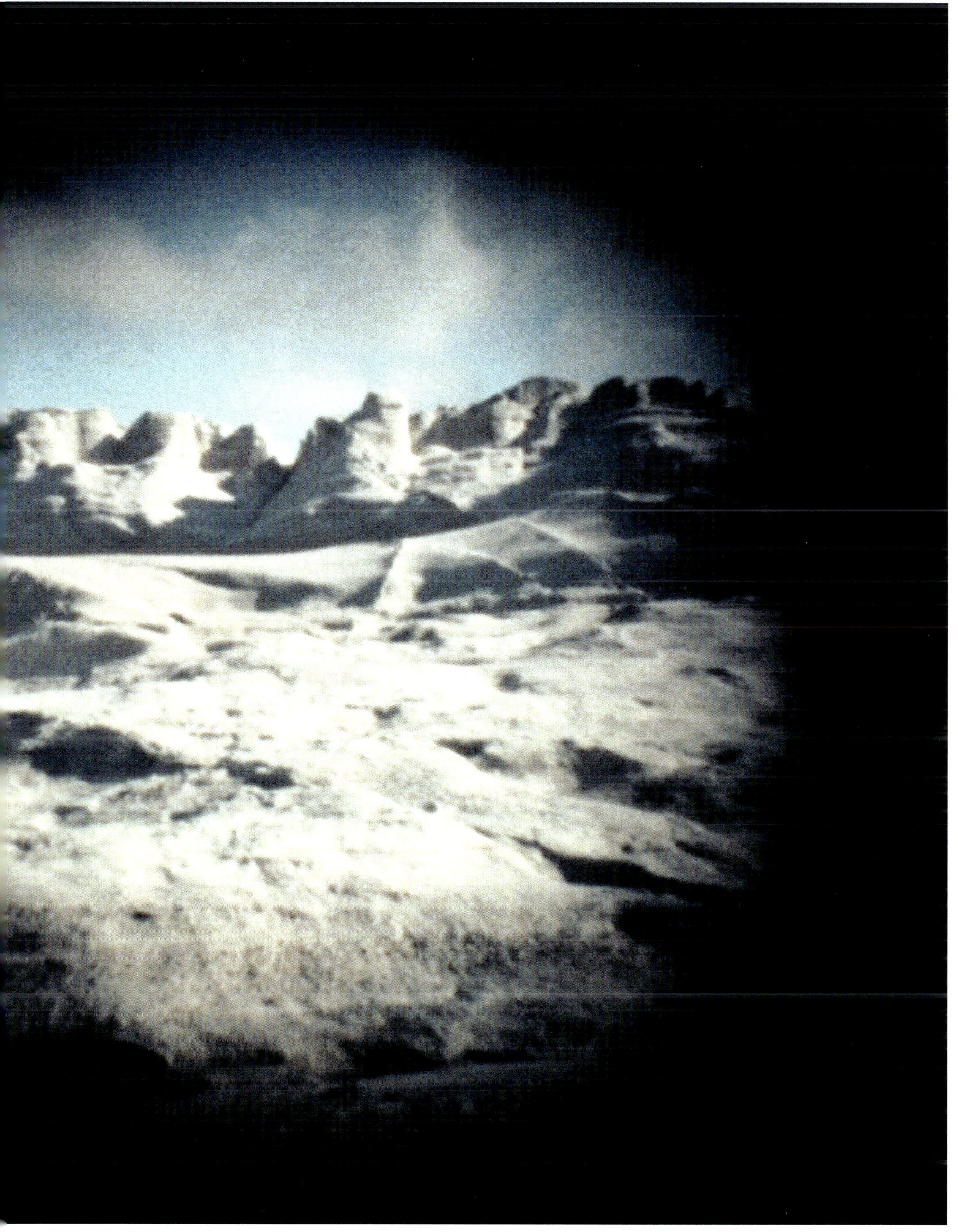

P.32 *13 Essential Rules for Understanding the World*, 2011.
Super 8mm film transferred to full HD video, 5:16 minutes.
Courtesy of the artist and Gypsum Gallery, Cairo.

P.36 *Eternity*, 2018. Acrylic, vinyl, and text, dimensions variable.
Commissioned by University Galleries of Illinois State University.
Courtesy of the artist.

P.40 *The Dent*, 2014. Super 16mm film transferred to full HD video,
19:02 minutes. Commissioned by the Abraaj Group Art Prize 2014.
Courtesy of the artist.

P.48 *The Many Colors of the Sky Radiate Forgetfulness*, 2014.
Super 16mm film transferred to full HD video, 11:09 minutes.
Courtesy of the artist and Gypsum Gallery, Cairo.

P.56 *The Everyday Ritual of Solitude Hatching Monkeys*, 2014.
Super 16mm film transferred to full HD video, 13:22 minutes.
Commissioned by Art in General, New York in collaboration with HOME,
Manchester. Courtesy of the artist and artSümer, Istanbul.

P.62 *We're All Victims of Our Own Adopted Fantasies Here (reprise)*, 2017.
5 C-prints from chemically altered slides on metallic Fujiflex paper.
150 x 47 cm overall. Collection of Belinda de Gaudemar, New York.

P.68 *Crystal Ball*, 2013. Double Super 8mm film transferred to HD video,
7:00 minutes. Courtesy of the artist and hunt kastner, Prague.

P.76 *No Shooting Stars*, 2016. Super 16mm film and GIF animations transferred
to full HD video, 14:25 minutes. Co-commissioned by Jeu de Paume, Paris, Fonda-
tion Nationale des Arts Graphiques et Plastiques and CAPC musée d'art contemporain de Bordeaux. Courtesy of the artist and Gypsum Gallery, Cairo.

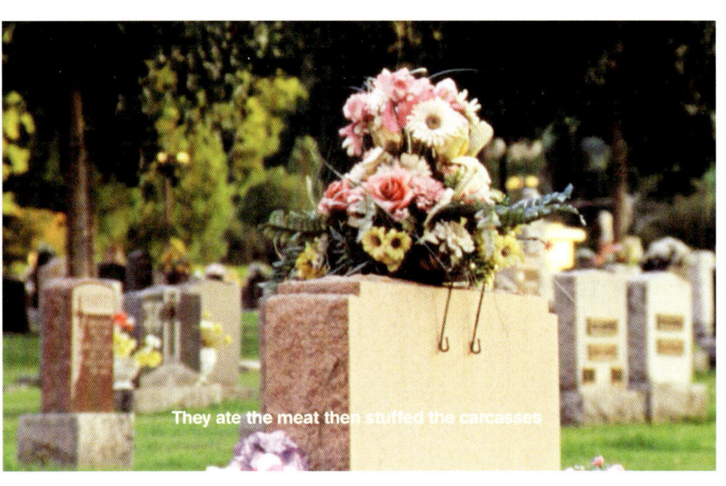
They ate the meat then stuffed the carcasses

ARTIST BIOGRAPHY

Basim Magdy (born: 1977, Assiut, Egypt) lives and works between Basel and Cairo. His work has been featured in recent solo exhibitions at MAAT Museum of Art, Architecture and Technology, Lisbon; La Kunsthalle Mulhouse, France; artSümer, Istanbul (2019); South London Gallery, London; Gypsum Gallery, Cairo (with Magdy El-Gohary); University Galleries of Illinois State University, Normal; Project Space Art Jameel, Dubai (2018); Arnolfini, Bristol; Mathaf, Doha; hunt kastner, Prague (2017); Museum of Contemporary Art, Chicago; CAPC Museum of Contemporary Art, Bordeaux; MAXXI National Museum of the 21st Century Arts, Rome; Jeu de Paume, Paris; Deutsche Bank KunstHalle, Berlin; and Z33 House for Contemporary Art, Hasselt (2016). Magdy's work has been included in the following biennials, as well as group exhibitions at: Museum of Modern Art, New York; Royal Academy, London; AnnexM, Athens; Akbank Sanat, Istanbul; Musée de Pully, Pully (2019); Athens Biennial 6, Athens; Galeria Municipal do Porto, Porto; Les Ateliers de Rennes—Biennale d'art contemporain 6, Rennes; South London Gallery, London; Le Fresnoy, Tourcoing (2018); GIBKA—Göteborg International Biennial for Contemporary Art, Gothenburg; Sharjah Biennial 13, Sharjah; Centre Pompidou, Paris; Castello di Rivoli, Torino; Hessel Museum of Art, Bard College, Annandale-on-Hudson (2017); Qalandiya International, Ramallah; Whitechapel Gallery, London; Salt Ulus, Ankara (2016); Museum of Modern Art, New York; New Museum Triennial, New York; Utah Museum of Contemporary Art, Salt Lake City; Museum of Contemporary Photography, Chicago; Garage Museum of Contemporary Art, Moscow; KW Institute for Contemporary Art, Berlin; Prague National Gallery, Prague; Museum of Modern Art, Warsaw; Flinders University Museum of Art, Adelaide (2015); La Biennale de Montreal, Montreal; SeMA Seoul Mediacity Biennale (2014); Istanbul Biennial 13; Sharjah Biennial 11 (2013); and La Triennale, Palais de Tokyo, Paris (2012), among others. Magdy's films have been screened at Tate Modern, London; Locarno Film Festival, Locarno; New York Film Festival, New York; International Film Festival Rotterdam, Rotterdam; and Institute of Contemporary Arts, London, among others. He was shortlisted for the Future Generation Art Prize, Kiev (2012) and was awarded the Abraaj Art Prize, Dubai (2014); New:Vision Award, CPH:DOX Film Festival, Copenhagen (2014); and the Experimental Award, Curtas Vila do Conde–International Film Festival, Portugal (2015). He was selected as the Deutsche Bank Artist of the Year (2016).

www.basimmagdy.com

ACKNOWLEDGMENTS

I first encountered Basim Magdy's work in *Surround Audience* at the New Museum in 2015. I walked into a projection space in the middle of *The Dent* and was completely mesmerized by the filmic transformations and mysterious narrative. I watched through to the end and found out about the circus elephant, then sat through its entirety to soak up as much as I could, and then immediately looked up the artist. When I learned that he was from Cairo and living in Basel, I didn't expect to meet him anytime soon. However, he came to Chicago for a residency the next year at the Hyde Park Art Center, where we had a studio visit that felt like it could have extended for several more hours. It was in that initial meeting that the first ideas toward this exhibition and publication began to take shape. The next few years allowed us the space to imagine both an exhibition and publication primarily focused on Magdy's work with analogue film and absurd text, which also included *Eternity*, whose painted gradient brilliantly illuminated our street-facing windows 24-hours per day.

I am grateful to the inimitable Bruce Jenkins for his early (and continued) excitement about the project, his scholarly contributions to our public conversation, and his sharp and incisive essay for this book. I am thankful to designer Engy Aly for her clear understanding of the needs of this work and for shaping this vibrant publication. Thank you to Belinda de Gaudemar for her generous loan of *We're All Victims of Our Own Adopted Fantasies Here (reprise)* for the exhibition. We are pleased to include Stan Brakhage's film stills thanks to the support of Fred Camper, Marilyn Brakhage, and the Estate of Stan Brakhage. We greatly appreciate the support of Kacha Kastner and Camille Hunt at hunt kastner, Prague; Aleya Hamza at Gypsum Gallery, Cairo; and Asli Sumer at artSümer, Istanbul. Thank you to the Alice and Fannie Fell Trust and the Illinois Arts Council Agency for making this exhibition possible.

This project represented a significant undertaking at a time when our organization was undergoing some transitions. I am incredibly grateful to the dedicated and talented graduate and undergraduate student assistants: Zach Buckley, Sheldon Gooch, Camila Pasquel, Janella Punzalan, and Trisha Wulf, and to alumnus Jason Hoffman of Jason Hoffman Studios, without all of whom this exhibition could not have come together. They were such a supportive and high-spirited team who worked hard and kept us laughing. Katie Barko provided exceptional student workshops, which included interactions via #dearbasim. I also appreciate the installation assistance provided by volunteers Marisa Boyd, Jenny Castanon, Kirsten Heteji, Emily Lehman, and Jake Murray, and the exhibition documentation by photographers Jason Reblando and Zach Buckley. Thank you to Stephanie Kohl Ringle for proofreading promotional materials and this publication. Eric Yeager, Matt Gromer, and Seth Engeman in our Wonsook Kim College of Fine Arts' technology unit provided sound advice and support, while Laura Primozic George and Alex Roehm in the Wonsook Kim School of Art graciously assisted in the final push before the opening. Thank you to Lisa Lofgren, University Galleries' Registrar, for cheerfully and effectively diving into the job mid-exhibition, and to Jean Miller, Dean of the Wonsook Kim College of Fine Arts, and Michael Wille, Director of the Wonsook Kim School of Art, for their continued support and encouragement. Lastly, thank you to Basim for sharing his vision, trusting us with his work, being a wonderful and flexible collaborator, and for pointing out that "time shrinks into a shapeshifting soap bubble floating."

— Kendra Paitz, Director and Chief Curator

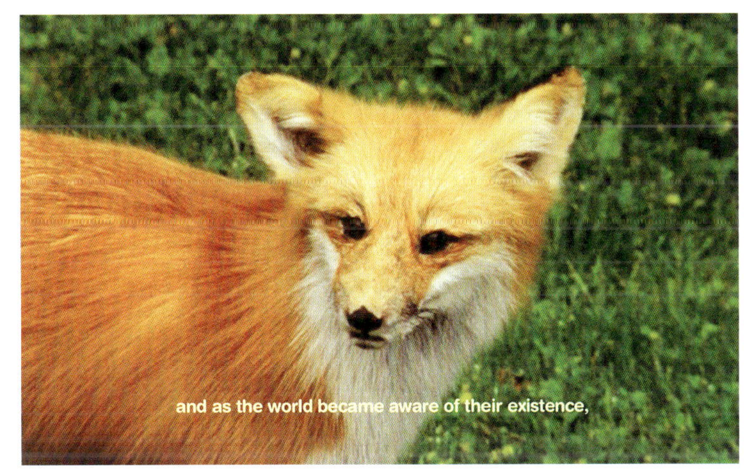
and as the world became aware of their existence,

CREDITS

This catalogue was published in conjunction with *Basim Magdy: To Hypnotize Them With Forgetfulness*, organized by Director and Chief Curator Kendra Paitz and presented at University Galleries of Illinois State University from October 26 through December 16, 2018.

The exhibition and publication were made possible by grants from the Alice and Fannie Fell Trust and the Illinois Arts Council Agency. Thank you to hunt kastner, Prague; Gypsum Gallery, Cairo; and artSümer, Istanbul for their support.

© 2019 University Galleries of Illinois State University. All rights reserved.
© 2019 *7 Essential Thoughts for Understanding Basim Magdy's Reimagination of the Camera Arts*, Bruce Jenkins
© 2019 *Mildly (or Wildly) Dystopian to Darkly Humorous: Basim Magdy and Kendra Paitz in Conversation*, Kendra Paitz and Basim Magdy

Photo credits: Jason Reblando, installation views, pages 36-37, 65, and 72; Zachary Buckley, installation view, page 79.

All reproductions of artwork © Basim Magdy.

PUBLISHER University Galleries of Illinois State University
EDITOR Kendra Paitz
DESIGNER Engy Aly
PRINTER Curtis 1000, Bloomington, Illinois
DISTRIBUTOR Distributed Arts Publishers, New York, New York – artbook.com
ISBN 978-0-945558-43-9

92

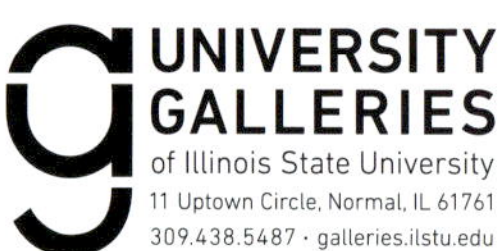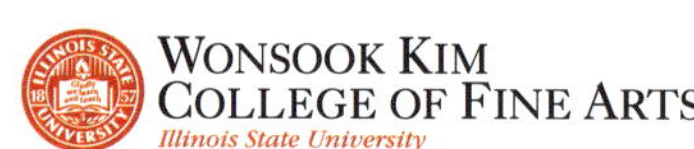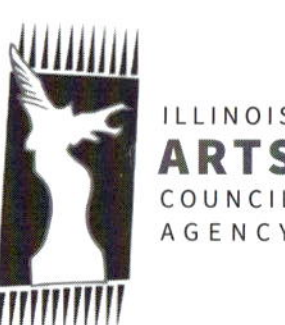

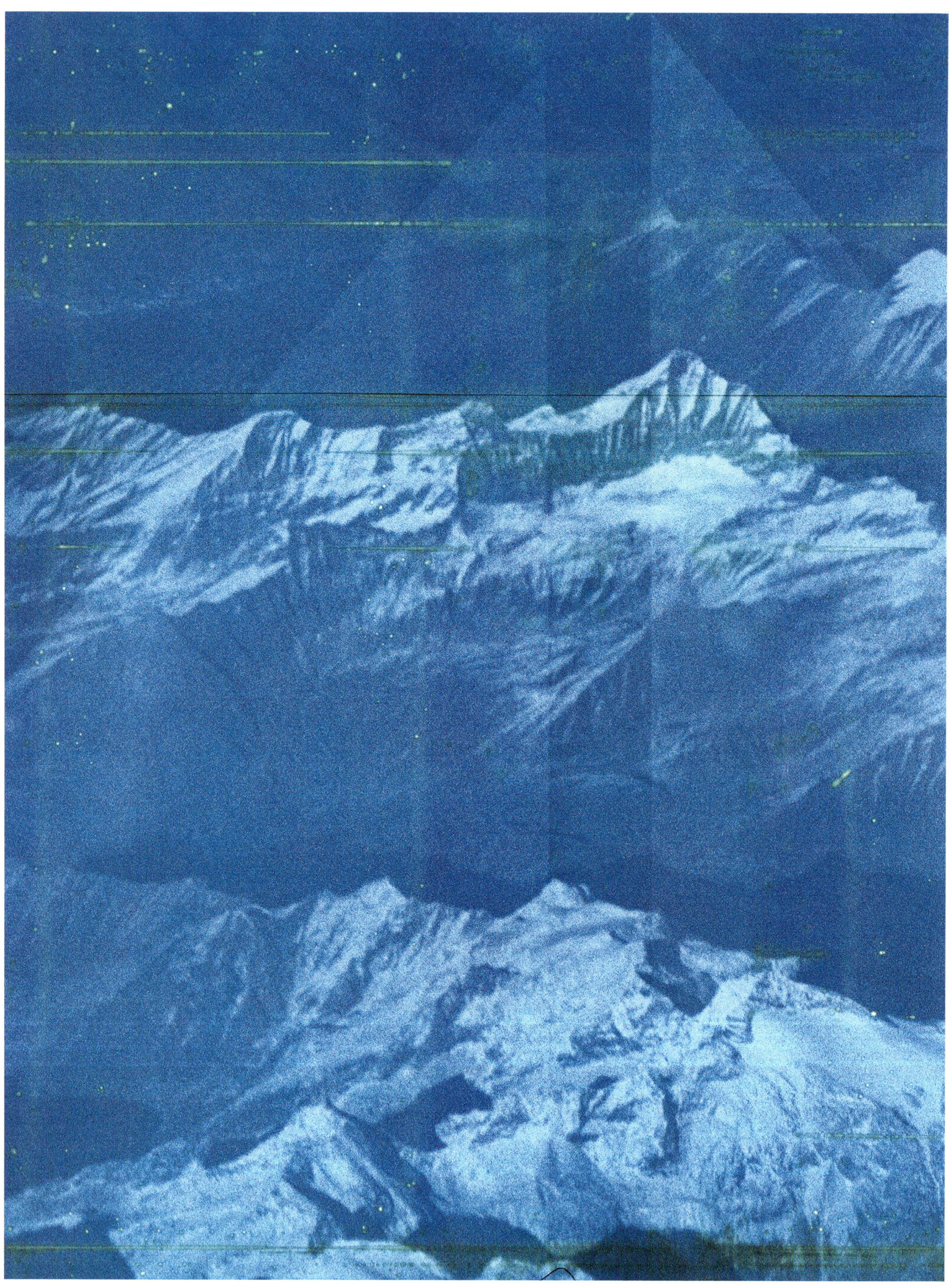

THE CIRCUS ELEPHANT
CAUGHT A GLIMPSE
OF ITS OWN REFLECTION
IN A WATER PUDDLE.
VANITY OF VANITIES.
EVERY CELL IN ITS GIANT
BODY REALIZED THE
NEW ENTRAPMENT WAS
NOTHING BUT A SIGN
FROM THE ELDERS.
AN ENDLESS DIAMOND
ROAD SURFACED ON THE
HORIZON. SOMETHING
HAD TO BE DONE.

An excerpt from the script of *The Dent*, 2014.

BASIM MAGDY WOULD LIKE TO DEDICATE THIS BOOK

TO LEILA AND HANNAH